Lid Off th[...]
A Wicc[...]

Patricia Crowther

Lid Off the Cauldron

©1998 Patricia Crowther

ISBN 186163 048 4

ALL RIGHTS RESERVED

First published 1981
Reprinted 1985, 1989, 1992
This revised edition first published 1998

The jacket illustration was painted by John Harper, who continues the tradition of the Plant Bran, the Hereditary Craft Family of the late Ruth Wynn-Owen.

Cover design by Paul Mason

Published by:

Capall Bann Publishing
Auton Farm,
Milverton,
Somerset
TA4 1NE

Contents

Acknowledgements

The author wishes to thank the following for their help and encouragement during the production of this book: Mr. J. Edward Vickers O.B.E.; Mr. John H. Cutton; Mr. Nicholas Sandys; Mr. Chris Bray; Mr. Ian Lilleyman; Mr. Leon Dickens and Aerofilms Ltd; for provision of two photographs. Thanks are also due to Macmillan & Co. Ltd. for permission to quote from *The Ballad of the White Horse* by G. K. Chesterton.

Preface

The fantastic opinion that the world began about 4000 BC has only recently been debunked. Christianity, or rather, 'Churchianity', has kept its children bound in swaddling clothes of religious dogma and questioning minds drugged with soporific ingredients calculated to dispense with any rebellion of thought.

A 'holier than thou' attitude has generally been adopted as a cloak by those carrying out the Church's unpleasant business. Yet, the sinister aspects of its activities have all the ingredients of a horror story. Where people showed a spark of intelligence in thinking for themselves, or displayed allegiance to or sympathy for an older religion, the mask was dropped and those who did not conform were cruelly persecuted.

With the death-pangs of the dying Piscean Age people have been released from their mental and physical bonds with all the implications that this involves. As if suddenly escaping from years spent in a dark dungeon, they have grabbed at ideas to ease the mental hunger, regardless of whether they were wholesome or suitable for them. There has never before been a time in which so many diverse cults, sects and 'scenes' have been followed, nor a time which has seen a greater 'happening' in the field of drugs, dope-peddlars and practitioners of Black Magic .

Men and women have awakened from their stupor only to find that they are alone in the dark forest. They are no longer cared for by religious advisers, telling them what to think and do. Their swaddling clothes have finally rotted away and they are naked again, and in many ways wholly innocent. Unfortunately, the umbilical cord leading them back to their Mother has been lost. It is somewhere in the forest and it has to be found. They will have to search long and wisely to find it, ignoring all stray pieces of discarded twine which could ensnare them or lead them deeper into the dark wood. Once the silver cord is seen, glowing in the darkness, they are safe. For it will lead them out through the bramble-strewn forest into the light of their great spiritual rebirth in the Aquarian Age.

Reflections

Silent is the Circle,
Keeping its secrets within its boundaries -
They wait to be discovered -- hopefully,
By one who will revere and keep the Mysteries.

Take my hand and enter the sacred hollow;
Candles at each Gate mark with living flame
The elemental Lords.
Crown of the whole -- the Altar,
Solidifies the unique purpose of both Gods and men.

The Mirror -- echo of the Moon
Hangs watchful behind the silver curtain.
All may be revealed here of the soul's evolution -
Past, present and future -- all one,
As time is betrayed and the shining shield
Returns our present image, and with it -- knowledge.

'Lady of the Three Ways'; deign to look on me;
Open my inner vision as I look upon the magical shield.
Queen of the Astral realm, show thy servant her true Self.
In the dark of the Moon is revelation and revealing;
Queen of the Night, I invoke Thee to aid me in my quest.'

Patricia C. Crowther

1 Going to the Devil

It is now over forty years since the revival of witchcraft, or the Craft of the Wise, but it is very doubtful if the public at large have any greater comprehension of it than they had in earlier times. Of course, there are many people who have gained a deeper insight into this much-maligned subject, but these are in the minority, possessing an inborn curiosity or natural inclination for serious study.

Most people do not want to have their picture of a horrid old woman, stirring a cauldron of noxious ingredients, taken away from them. After all, this is the image which has been hammered into the subconscious minds of the public for hundreds of years, and they are reluctant to let go of it.

The medieval Church did its work extremely thoroughly. Witches worshipped the Devil, and the evil ones had to be routed out of the community and punished. Nothing was too bad for the creatures. The agonies of fire and torture would, perhaps, save their guilty souls from the perpetual fires of Hell!

The many ingenious ways and methods of torture were the creation of priestly minds obsessed with the idea of original sin: minds, which had been instilled with the horridness of sex and particularly of woman. Here was the viper! The female serpent who seduced and debased the heart and soul of man!

This is Catholic theology, and in the Roman Calendar one of the most acclaimed names is that of St Augustine. Yet, his vile, degrading opinions about the human body are loathsome. His famous epigram, *Inter faeces et urinam nascimur* (We are born between excrement and urine), reveals a cast of mind unbelievably squalid.

Other saints were no better. St Bernard proclaimed '*Man is nothing else than a foetid sperm, a sack of dung*', while St Jerome said of women,'*The food of worms, you have never seen a viler dung-hill. She is the gate by which the Devil enters; the road that leads to sin; she is what the sting of the scorpion is.....Woman is a fire, man the tow, and the Devil the bellows.*'

St Maximus, who died in AD 662, took a similar view of woman: '*She makes shipwreck of men, she is a tyrant who leads them captive, a lioness who holds them fast in her embraces, a siren decked out to lure them to destruction, a malicious evil beast.*'

St Anastasius the Sinaite saw her as '*a viper clothed with a shining skin, a comfort to the demons, a laboratory of devils, a flaming furnace, a javelin wherewith the heart is pierced, a storm by which houses are overthrown, a guide leading to darkness, a teacher of all evil, an unbridled tongue speaking evil of the saints.*'

We cannot dismiss all these opinions as mere nonsense, because they express views that are still the official law of the Church! These quotations, with others a great deal worse, come from the *Directorium Sacerdotale*, a guide for priests in their public and private life, published by Fr Benedict Valny, a French Jesuit, and approved by the Vatican.

The male-dominated religion of Christianity, sterile, oppressive and guilt-ridden, had turned inwards upon itself and the result was cruelty and sadism. This was the obvious release for pent-up sexual energy, deprived of a natural outlet: a very far cry from its innocent founder, Jesus Christ, who

6

would have been utterly stricken to observe the barbaric ways of men, making declarations in His name.

The negative pattern was given a good boost through the Devil, or Old Nick. His conception was far from being a pure one. He could be described as a spiritual homunculus put together from various pre-Christian god forms - at least according to his supposed 'physical' appearance. In point of fact, there never was a description of His Satanic Majesty prior to the Middle Ages, but since that time, we have seen his spectacular figure occurring in every conceivable form of art.

Many pictures show the Devil seated upon a high throne amidst his devotees who are indulging in every kind of debauchery. This theme also reflects the subconscious mind of men, long indoctrinated with hostile dogma, concerning natural, bodily functions.

It was commonly assumed that the Devil's servants were, of course, the witches. The contempt of the Christian Church for women was beneficent compared with its opinion of the adherents of the Old Religion. The emphasis on the concept of a Mother Goddess attended by priestesses could not, at any price, be allowed to continue; and the price turned out to be very high - namely human blood!

The first hint of the coming storm came in the form of a document called the *Canon Episcopi* of AD 906 published by Regino in his *De Ecclesiastica Disciplinis*. He ascribed it to the Church Council of Ancyra, which assembled in AD 314, though modern authorities question this. It reads like a fairy tale compared with the later *Malleus Maleficarum*, which came to be known as the 'Witch Hammer'.

Whatever the origins of the *Episcopi*, it was used as an official document by the Christian Church. Its main assertion was that witches were heretics who worshipped 'Diana, the Goddess of the Pagans', as the following extract shows:

It is also not to be omitted that some wicked women perverted by the devil, seduced by illusions and phantasms of demons, believe and profess themselves, in the hour of night, to ride upon certain beasts with Diana, the goddess of pagans, and an innumerable multitude of women, and in the silence of the dead of night, to traverse great space of earth, and to obey her commands as of their mistress, and to be summoned to her service on certain nights. But I wish it were they alone who perished in their faithlessness, and did not draw many with them into the destruction of infidelity. For an innumerable multitude, deceived by this false opinion, believe this to be true and, so believing, wander from the right faith and are involved in the error of pagans when they think that there is anything of divinity or power except the one God. Wherefore the priests throughout their churches should preach with all insistence to the people that they may know this to be in every way false and that such phantasms are imposed on the minds of infidels and not by the divine but by the malignant spirit.

This not so subtle propaganda was put out with the intention of frightening people away from the Old Religion. In some cases it may have worked, but it was apparently overlooked that most of the populace in those days could neither read nor write! These accomplishments were limited to the upper classes, the rich and those in the Church itself.

The clergy had to work overtime to instill these views into their flocks. Even so, to change people's faith is practically impossible. The only way it can be done successfully is by force, and this is what, in the end, the Church had to use in order to achieve any kind of victory.

So, in 1484 Pope Innocent VIII published a Papal Bull (a good description) that hit out in no uncertain terms at the witches.

8

It was claimed that witches copulated with demons in the forms of incubi and succubi; killed babies, cattle and people, afflicted men and women with all kinds of diseases; prevented intercourse between man and wife; and made men impotent and women sterile. The edict was a signal for executioners everywhere to clean up their torture chambers and see that their instruments of pain were in working order.

The Bull was printed and disseminated all over Europe, and although there were plenty of convictions as a result of it, thousands of people continued attending their religious meetings and festivals.

Two years later, in 1486, the infamous *Malleus Maleficarum* was published under the Pope's patronage. The authors were Heinrich Kramer and Jakob Sprenger, whom the Pope called his 'beloved sons'. It was written specifically with the intention of being an official document for the persecution of the witches, and the silencing of any voices which may have been in their favour.

The *Canon Episcopi* had become an embarrassing document to the unrelenting exterminators of Paganism. How could anyone be convicted of witchcraft when it taught that all witchcraft was a delusion? The *Malleus Maleficarum* denied the doctrine of the previous work by stating it was a heresy *not* to believe in the fact of witchcraft, and provided adequate 'proof' of its evils.

There is the usual abuse of women and stories about people being carried off by demons who could kill men and women by a mere look or even by touching them, as well as about witches using the Host to work evil magic.

It has been pointed out by scholars that both these works were in fact, forgeries. (See *The Meaning of Witchcraft* by Gerald B. Gardner.)

To most people the Devil was a dangerously attractive figure , and many equated him with the pagan deity Pan, the virile, masculine concept of divinity, much beloved by all nations in Europe. To Christians in general, he was evil personified. The naíveté of the Church in building up this gigantic thought-form is transparently obvious to serious students of the occult. It was, indeed, a magical image of immense proportions, and like most astral entities which have been brought to 'birth' in hatred, it proceeded to take control of its creators!

Even in this so-called enlightened age, the Church is still waging 'war' upon witchcraft, spiritualism and the like. The training of priests in exorcism is now the 'in' thing, although this is part of a priest's instruction prior to ordination.

It seems there are more and more people 'possessed' by evil spirits through 'dabbling' in witchcraft and Black Magic. In modern psychological terms, a so-called 'possessed' person would be said to be suffering from some mental disturbance not 'evil spirits'. His treatment would probably involve suitable therapy and medical attention, not a bodily exorcism.

The Craft of the Wise will not admit anyone who is in the slightest degree unstable. It's adherents are generally intelligent, well read, and humane people. Furthermore, it would be hard to find a person who has not benefited from the Craft's erudite, comprehensive, spiritual teachings, and who has not become a better individual through his or her allegiance to it.

The facts are that in this Christian country more than half of the hospitals are filled with people suffering from some form of mental disorder. Witches? I think not !

As for the bogey of Black Magic, this is a phrase often used indiscriminately and wildly. Real Black Magic is the use of the powers of the mind with the intention of harming another being in some way. Any person who thinks evil against another is performing an act of Black Magic. A witch or 'wise one' would be very careful what he or she did in this direction, believing in the Universal Law of Karma. This is the principle that 'As you sow; so will you reap', and is much older than Christian teachings.

In the Craft there are few laws, but the ones which exist are closely connected with magic and are positive, and life-affirming:

> *Eight words the Wiccan Ride fulfil:*
> *An it harm none, do what ye will.*

Therefore, if a witch *did* intentionally set out to harm anyone, he (or she) would not only be breaking a very strict law, thus incurring the wrath of the Goddess, but would also be putting himself (or herself) in jeopardy, as the magic performed would rebound on them three-fold.

It is quite evident that people versed in the practice of magic, can quite easily 'overlook' another person, *if they wished to do so*. The facts are that being, or becoming *wise*, and knowing what they know, they steer well clear of doing such harm, being quite sure of the consequences of such an act. In any case, why take on someone else's faults? Presumably a person must have been 'put out' or hurt by another, to make them want to hit back. The Wise Ones allow those at fault to expiate their own negative Karma.

It has been known that if someone really sets out to harm a member of the Craft in some way, the Coven has worked to build up a psychic wall of protection for them, and this has been successfully accomplished. More, they will not do. People who *do* indulge in hostile thoughts and make a habit of it are usually morose, selfish individuals, whose thoughts have made them so - remembering that 'thoughts are things'.

In other words, everyone makes their own particular Heaven or Hell for themselves.

Since the renaissance of the Old Religion, thousands of people have written to the witches for help, and, in a great many cases, provided the pleas have sounded genuine, they have been able to grant these requests. The work is not easy; it requires an unselfish approach to life in order to concentrate on someone they have most probably never met. Their successes are not coincidences. A coincidence is a thing similar to the incident itself, and can happen once or twice, but after that it is definitely something else. All in all, magic can be fairly described as 'the art of getting results'.

It is really the scoffing attitude of the mass media to anything magical that has made witchcraft a laughing-stock, whereas, if Black Magic is mentioned, it is swallowed hook, line and sinker! If Black Magic is believed in, why not White Magic? The answer is very simple; Black Magic is much more exciting especially when it is suitably embroidered by the sensation writers: sex, sacrificial blood rites and the ravishing of virgins (if you can find one),appeal to the carnal appetites of certain sections of the public.

Today we are seeing the effects of repression caused by puritanical thinking and behaviour. Don't let us deceive ourselves; this is the root cause behind the so-called permissive society. The people who are at the back of pornography, sadism and violence of every description are the end-product of generations of repression. Both forms of thinking are equally bad. It is only when we come to the realisation that sex is a natural function, not divorced or different from any other bodily activity that we shall see any improvement in our spiritual evolution.

To our ancestors, who worshipped the Great Goddess and Her consort the Horned God, sex was regarded as sacred. We cannot do better than follow their lead. They held woman in high esteem, as the blessed life-giver and sustainer. In many ways she was regarded as the wiser. more sagacious of the sexes. She embodied all mystery and magic, and by giving her this allegiance, man sanctified and purified himself.

This very ancient idea can be seen mirrored in the Orders of Chivalry, and in the quest of the Knights for the Holy Grail. An even earlier concept was the Cauldron of Cerridwen and of Immortality, which yielded three drops of the Grace of Inspiration. There is a mystery here which has to be re-discovered.

To many scholars, the Grail is thought not to have been a metal object, but something far more sublime: perhaps the perfect virginal woman, fit to be the Mother of the Divine Babe. Perhaps communion with the divine Goddess was the goal. A study of the Grail legends, however, will show the very high spiritual and moral standards of our forebears.

The renaissance of the Old Religion points the way. The flame has been re-kindled in the Cauldron. The message for the future is clear; *We must spring again from the Craft.*

2 The Renaissance

Ever since the Roman invasion of Britain, there has been a steady decline of esoteric knowledge. The Romans destroyed most of the evidence of our spiritual heritage, which up to that time, flourished like the bay tree.

This knowledge was concerned, among other things, with the powers of Nature and the ways in which they can be utilized for the benefit of the human being. The ancient Ley Lines are an example. These lines, which form a network all over the world and converge on places where the power crosses, are indicated on the surface of the ground by straight tracks, stone circles, monoliths and hill-figures. The Christians built their churches on these sacred places. Whether they knew the secret, or merely built on spots which were sacred to the Old Religion, is not known.

The Ley power itself is literally the energy which causes everything to grow. It is activated at certain times of the year, i.e. in spring and summer. But not all the lines are of this quickening power. Some of them indicate water, which can be found by dowsing with a divining rod.

Alfred Watkins was the first person to discover them in the 1920s. It happened in a very remarkable way. One hot summer's day he was riding across the Bredwardine hills, near Hereford, and he stopped to admire the view. Suddenly, the whole landscape seemed to change and he was looking at a part of the country as it was in some far-off age. His eyes beheld a web of lines stretching as far as the eye could see. The places where the lines crossed were marked by stones, holy wells, cairns and stone circles. The whole panorama lay before him in this breathtaking moment of heightened perception. Watkins was a highly respected figure in Hereford, where he transacted business as a merchant. He had become interested in pre-history and ancient sites, and his vision led him to mark out the sites on a 1-inch Ordnance Survey map. The result was a confirmation of what he had 'seen', and was echoed all over Britain.

The ancient places, when marked with a ruler, flowed in straight lines. A peculiar feature was the appearance of certain names which occurred frequently along the ways, or tracks. Particularly, 'Cold', 'Merry', 'Dod' and 'Ley', which resulted in Watkins calling them Ley Lines. His book, *The Old Straight Track*, caused a minor sensation, especially in the archaeological field. It was something which had been discovered through senses other than the 'normal' ones, and was,therefore, suspect. Nevertheless, it lead to a society being formed by his supporters, called the Straight Track Postal Club.

Watkins and his friends became convinced that there was something more to the lines than that of direction. They perceived that animals and birds followed them during migration. It was also discovered that there were similar systems of tracks in other countries of the world. It was concluded that they been made over currents of energy which had been known to ancient man and had resulted in the laying out of a physically illustrated guide. Alfred Watkins died on 5 April 1935, but he left a precious heritage which is of inestimable value for those with eyes to see.

Following Watkins's work, further progress has broadened the concept of the Ley Lines considerably. Guy Underwood, an archaeologist and dowser, wrote *The Pattern of the Past* and in *The View Over Atlantis*, John Michell describes the esoteric engineering techniques which were used to build monuments such as Stonehenge and the Pyramids. He shows how celestial harmony, astronomy, solar geometry and the Magic Square all combined in the erection of ancient monuments and stone circles. A companion volume, *The City of Revelation*, discusses the proportion and symbolic numbers of the Cosmic Temple.

The tide of interest and investigation into what had hitherto been shrouded in mystery and ignorance continued to gather momentum. The subtle energies in both humans and plants received attention from the pioneer work of T. C. Lethbridge. Of his many books, *Ghosts and the Divining Rod* is of particular interest, while his fascinating *E.S.P., Beyond Time and Distance*, demonstrates that the mind of man is immortal and outside the influence of both time and space.

Lethbridge's observations are remarkable, in that he seems to have discovered the existence of a previously unknown type of ray which is made use of by birds in migration and by animals. His investigations were the result of the actions of a Privet Hawk moth, which entered his house for reasons other than shelter!

Professor Gerald S. Hawkins has made an extensive and remarkable study of Stonehenge (the Hanging Stones) making use of a modern computer. His work has been published in *Stonehenge Decoded* and reveals how the ancient people of Britain constructed an edifice which was both an instrument and a work of art. All the available data on its alignments was fed into a computer and found to be accurate, despite the fact that the odds against this have been calculated to be 10,000 to 1. Stonehenge is aligned to the rising and setting of both the Sun and the Moon at the solstices and equinoxes, and it could also have been used to predict eclipses. In the Professor's own words: "Stonehenge is locked to the Sun and Moon as tightly as the tides".

All these amazing discoveries have occurred in the Cycle of the Moon. According to astrology (another very ancient science), each planet rules in turn, for a period of thirty-six years, and this is known as a Cycle. The Moon Cycle commenced in 1945 we were under the influence of that mysterious orb until 1981.

The renaissance of witchcraft, with its worship of the Moon Goddess, happened, strangely enough, at the beginning of the Moon Cycle. Its approach was heralded some years earlier by a book by that eminent scholar Dr Margaret Murray entitled *Witchcraft in Western Europe*. This work was one of the first this century to show witchcraft as a religion. It discusses the witch-trials in great detail, together with the beliefs, initiation ceremonies and rituals. There is also a comprehensive list, from the fifteenth to the seventeenth centuries, of covens, the names of the members, and the names of lone witches, from all parts of the British Isles.

At the beginning of the Moon Cycle, a little known novel, *A Goddess Arrives* was published. This was written by Gerald B. Gardner, a man who was to have a tremendous influence upon the renaissance of witchcraft. He followed it with *High Magic's Aid* written under the name, Scire, a story that contained much information about the beliefs and practices of the witches, including a very interesting magical invocation.

In 1952, Margaret Murray's *The God of the Witches* showed that the witches of olden times were not half-crazed lunatics. Indeed, such well-known historical figures as Joan of Arc and King Edward III were mentioned in connection with the Old Religion.

1954 saw the publication of yet another work from the pen of Gerald Gardner, *Witchcraft Today*. However, this book differed in one important respect from his previous ones: this time he admitted that he was an initiated member of the Craft and described ceremonies and practises which had hitherto been kept secret, mainly because of the *Witchcraft Act*. But this Act had been repealed in 1951 and replaced by the *Fraudulent Mediums Act* which, as its title shows, proves the existence of *genuine* mediums!

Witchcraft Today sold very well and has been re-printed many times. Gardner followed it up with yet another book, *The Meaning of Witchcraft*, which still continues to be popular. It was shortly after this book appeared that Robert Graves wrote an anthology, *The White Goddess*, which, he tells us, he was spiritually inspired to do. Soon other writers of repute added their quota of publications on the great antiquity of witch beliefs. The wheel was gathering momentum, and appeared to be in the witches' favour. But was it? Bringing witchcraft out into the open again seems to have been a mixed blessing. Many genuine devotees believed, as did Gerald Gardner, that the general public ought to know the true facts about it. They were confident that the time had come to inform people that there was no connection with Devil worship and that there never had been. Modern witches felt that if their predecessors had endured the agonies of torture and cruel death, they could put up with a few jeers, a sometimes hostile press, or a grilling, condescending interview on television or radio.

Many witches gave talks on their beliefs, and still do so. But certain people found there was money to be made from this intriguing subject. Dubious adverts began to appear in various occult magazines, insinuating perversions and inviting the gullible to join a particular 'witchcraft' group. 'Devil worship in Suburbia', screamed the headlines of the yellow press. Journalists cashed in on the 'new' sensation. Many of them wrote books and articles which were a hotch-potch of Satanism, Black Magic and Voodoo. All came under the same heading - 'Witchcraft'! Though to give journalists their due, there were some who took the trouble to study the subject and to interview members of the Craft. These writers gave unbiased views, but unfortunately, they were in the minority.

Many of the present day covens were founded by gerald Gardner. Others have been formed by people who became members of the original ones and who were eventually entitled to form covens of their own.

Every person who wishes to become a member of the Craft must be brought in by an already initiated witch, otherwise the initiation is not valid. This has been a strict law in the Craft all down the ages. Yet, strangely enough, a few witches began a slur campaign against Gardner by announcing that they were 'hereditary' witches i.e. from witch families and calling Gardner's covens 'Gardnerians', presumably inferring that all but themselves were fakes. This rather amused the present writer who knew the people who made the attacks and had even worked with them in one of Gardner's covens. They were, in fact, initiates of Gardner.

There are, of course, many witch families where the knowledge has been passed down from generation to generation. But it should be pointed out that although this is an admirable way for one to enter the Hollow Mysteries, it is not the *only* way. One of the chief tenets of the Craft - and indeed many other pagan religions - is a firm belief in reincarnation. The witches believe that if you have been a witch in a previous life, you can, when re-born, be drawn back to it. Therefore there are at least two ways of inheriting the wisdom: by being born into a witch family, or by being reincarnated and initiated into a present-day coven.

People belonging to hereditary groups, while not wishing to come out into the open themselves, are by no means against those witches who do. I have received many communications from them congratulating me on my fearlessness in defending the Faith, while keeping my vows concerning its secrets. They fully acknowledge that the Craft must be kept alive at all costs, and that the only way to do this is to introduce new blood into it.

They told me that the return of the Goddess had been prophesied for some considerable time. In the new age of Aquarius, the feminine principle of Divinity would again come into Her own. There was to be a future time of happiness and peace on earth, when the doctrine of a wholly male god would give way to true equality of male and female in Godhead. and woman, under the guidance of the Goddess, would resume her rightful position as priestess and prophetess

The physical aspect of the Goddess, that of Mother Nature, is already beginning, albeit a little late, to command respect. The recent forming of a society for the conservation of the environment indicates that people are beginning to realise that the survival of all life depends on natural resources. It is to be hoped that we are not too late to improve the situation. As Robert Graves says in *The White Goddess*, 'the longer the Goddess is ignored, the sterner will Her mask become'.

The Moon Cycle occurred near the end of the Age of Pisces, an Age lasting approximately 2,000 years. The Age of Aquarius begins around the year 2,080, although some authorities say it has already begun. However, it is probable that each Age overlaps and merges into the next.

I believe the Aquarian birth-pangs have already begun. The tumult and dissatisfaction in the world, and the complete disregard of old ideas and dogmas, seem to point this way. On the other hand, however, there are new ideas and concepts emerging which are expressive of the characteristics of the sign, Aquarius. One of the greatest of these attributes is freedom of the soul; to be 'as free as air' is a good synonym. It will bring forth 'free thinking', and man's most spiritual and humane qualities. It seems clear that the renaissance of the Craft of the Wise is a breath of fresh air; the first light breeze which precedes the Wind of Aquarius!

3 In Quest of the Ancient Gods of Britain

It seems very strange that in almost every country of the world, with the sole exception of Britain, there is carefully documented evidence of the people's earliest religious beliefs and teachings. Or the ancient traditions have been given orally and passed down in this way in the form of stories and legends of the past.

Outstanding examples are Greece and Egypt, which are, even today, given extreme reverence and respect. There is little doubt that they were important centres of high culture and religious thought. Nevertheless, the argument is not how great *they* were, but why it is assumed that the Ancient Britons were illiterate savages!

It is incredible to think that up to the last few years this idea was deliberately fostered and instilled into the minds of our children, from a very early age. It is hard to believe that no-one questioned this nonsense, and that if they had, they would probably have met with a cynical stare, or a shrug of the shoulders. yet, this utterly erroneous idea has been fostered by the Establishment for hundreds of years.

The Guide to English History, by the Rev. Dr Bewer, states that the Romans introduced Roman dress, manners and laws to the naked savages (the Britons), although before the Roman invasion, British merchants walked the streets of Rome and sailed to Italian ports with their exports of cattle, silver, iron, corn and tin! The Abbé de Fontenu explained that the Phoenicians had established a trade route with Britain before 1190 B.C., and Professor Boyd Dawkins wrote about their many industries such as spinning, glass-making, weaving, pottery and bronze-working, as well as the most admirable carpentry.

Anyone with a grain of commonsense must realize that a nation's heritage is not discarded by its people. They are only too eager to relate the history of their country, and are usually very proud to do so. There must be another reason for the view that the Ancient Britons were savages!

When a nation is turned into a totalitarian state, either by conquest or by any other occurrence, its people lose their independence of thought and action. In other words, they have to keep in line, and their behaviour patterns are moulded to the designs of their leaders.

Though they still display various talents and aptitudes, these are strictly controlled by the state. Any special genius or intelligence is used for the purposes of the state, and any benefits from these qualities go to the furtherance of the state and *not* to the individuals themselves.

The people of Britain have held democratic views from the very earliest times. Three of the oldest laws covered, 'protection of the old, protection of the babe, and protector of the foreigner who cannot speak the British tongue' and these have been regenerated in the present century. But with so much pro-Roman, anti-British propaganda hurled with ferocity against these islands for hundreds of years, it is small wonder that it is such a difficult task to uncover our religious heritage.

The burning down of the great library at Bangor Abbey, and the subsequent persecutions of the Druids and the witches makes it hard to obtain a true picture of the past. Many people must have died without passing their beliefs on, although it is said that nothing is completely lost but is stored in what Carl Gustav Jung called the 'collective unconscious' of a race or people.

Winston Churchill was, perhaps, the only voice in recent years to be heard on the subject. In his famous address to the US Congress during the Second World War, he declared: 'He must indeed have a blind soul who cannot see that some Great Purpose or Design is being worked out here below, of which we have the honour to be faithful servants.'

It was Winston Churchill who had the Stone of Destiny removed from beneath the Coronation Chair in Westminster Abbey and taken to a place of safety for the duration of the war. The Stone is said to be the one upon which Jacob laid his head, while on the plains of Luz. In its long, sacred history it has been taken to Egypt, Spain, Ireland and Scotland, from whence it was brought to London by Edward I. It is recorded that the Stone was always used at the crowning of kings and is considered to be a most venerable relic. (See *The Stone of Destiny* by F Wallace Connon.)

Churchill also gave the order that the ravens in the Tower of London must be looked after and fed at all costs, despite the apparently trivial nature of his instructions. This discloses his belief in the legends of our past. It is said that once the ravens desert their home in the Tower, it will presage the downfall of our Royal House and of our country.

The raven was the sacred bird of Bran the Blessed, one of the ancient god-kings of Britain. His visit to Ireland to rescue his sister, Branwen, ended in his death. But, while dying, he told his followers to cut off his head and take it back with them to the White Island and to bury it in the Bryn Gwynn, or White Mound, with its face to the East. While thus buried, there would be no invasion of Britain. It is said that the relic

24

was subsequently dug up and thereafter our island was beset by many invaders. The Tower of London now stands on this ancient mound, originally dedicated to the White Goddess.

The legend of Bran is one of eleven stories of Celtic genius making up the *Mabinogion*, which is regarded as a masterpiece of medieval European literature and which escaped the invaders' eagle eyes. These stories were translated by Lady Charlotte Guest in 1906, a second translation appearing in Everymans Library in 1970. Evangeline Walton adapted three of the legends in a most fascinating manner in, *The Island of the Mighty*, *The Children of Llyr* and *The Song of Rhiannon*. Some time ago a psychic message came through to me. Its main implication was that something would be discovered in the Tower of London and also in Windsor Castle that would reveal a part of our spiritual past.

More than a year later, a friend told me about an acquaintance of his who had been repairing the White Tower in the Tower of London after the explosion of a bomb. My friend was told that a secret room beneath the Tower had been discovered. It had the Pentagram or five-pointed star on each wall, which seems to point to the meeting-place of an occult society. The Pentagram is a universal magical symbol, but it is also used by witches! Could this room have been an old temple of the Royal Coven?

As far as I know, there was no publicity about this remarkable discovery. Perhaps a reader could throw more light on an intriguing puzzle?

To return to the Celts. Although their legends contain miraculous happenings, similar to those of Greece and elsewhere, the Celtic myths are much more wild and untamed. The same distinction can be seen in their stone carvings. It is realized that when religious art-forms become too refined and stylized, they lose the essential life-force which was present at their conception. The Celtic art-forms depict life very forcibly. They have a quality of living energy unlike any others

In the Roman baths at Bath, there is a fine Celtic carving of the God Lugh. It personifies the fiery, masculine energy of the Sun God, with hair and beard spread around him in 'tongues of flame'. The whole carving is surrounded by a circle of oak leaves and acorns. The oak is the oldest tree symbol of this god, known to man.

The museum authorities continue to call it 'The Gorgon's Head' despite repeated attempts by various people to correct this glaring error. Most of the public know the Gorgon to be of Greek origin and a <u>female </u>monster. This is only one of thousands of similar errors connected with our ancient beliefs. The same museum displays a stone carving of three women described as 'of unknown origin'. The Three Mothers, or the Three Ladies of Britain, is the oldest concept of the Trinity. The Goddess Triformis has three aspects: the Virgin, the Mother and the Crone which are represented, in a material form, by the new, full and waning Moon. Thus she is also Goddess of the Moon. There are numerous threefold statues in museums all over Britain classified as: 'Figures of unknown origin'.

There is also a bronze head of Minerva in the Bath museum. The Goddess has thousands of names according to locality, the Romans knowing her as Minerva. The head was discovered during excavations and dated at 1727. The Roman altar to Sulis Minerva is close to the main spring and source of the hot water which rises in the King's Bath. Unfortunately, the altar is boarded up and inaccessible to the general public, but the fact remains that the place has been sacred to the Goddess, whatever her name, throughout millennia.

The building of Christian churches upon pagan sacred sites is repeated all over Europe. St Paul's Cathedral in London was erected on an older temple dedicated to Diana, and beneath the Notre Dame in Paris an altar to Cernunnos, the Horned God, was found, which was used until well into the seventeenth century.

Michael Harrison, in *The Roots of Witchcraft*, writes about a very exciting find by Professor Geoffrey Webb, after the Second World War. It seems a bomb had displaced a huge stone slab which was covering the altar in an old church. Upon examination, he found, hidden inside the altar, a stone phallus. Professor Webb discovered that subsequent examinations in other churches disclosed similar stone phalli concealed within the altars. The estimate given was ninety per cent!

The phallus, as the giver of life, was used by followers of the Old Religion as a symbol of The God. The Lingam (or phallus) is still used in India today, along with the Yoni, a female symbol, for exactly the same reason. The retaining of the stone phalli within Christian altars shows that they were considered too powerful to be discarded, however abhorrent they seemed to the new priesthood.

The complement to the ritual phallus is a holed stone which symbolizes the Great Mother. Many of them have been found at the ancient site of Avebury in Wiltshire. They represent the Holy Vagina, the fount of all life, and the Gate of Re-birth. An extension of this symbol is the Sheila-na-Gig, usually translated as 'Mother of the God', though this is open to question. These carvings depict the Goddess squatting in a 'giving birth' position and displaying her genitalia. Representations can be seen at St Mary's Church, Whittlesford, Cambridgeshire; Oaksey Church, Cirencester and at Kilpeck Church, Herefordshire, although they are more numerous in Ireland.

We must view these symbols with the eyes of our ancestors, to whom sex was not a dirty word, but a sacred and beautiful act which identified them with the God and the Goddess, the creators of the universe. Otherwise, we are distorting the <u>truth</u> of the beliefs and profaning their religious objects. Discovering our spiritual heritage is no easy matter; for example it is only when actually bathing in the water of the King's Bath at Bath that you can read the stone inscription on the wall. This says that one Brutus, the great-grandson of Aeneas, of Troy, founded Bladden, now known as the city of Bath.

Brutus, the Trojan prince, is said to have journeyed to the Isle of Albion, or the White Islands of the Blessed, as Britain was then named, about 1103 BC. His arrival here is also commemorated by the Brutus Stone, in Totnes, Devon. This stone is now set in the pavement of Forre Street with the inscription, 'This is the Brutus Stone'

The story of Brutus and his royal line is one of the most romantic in our history, and one of the least known. The fall of Troy took place in 1183 BC. It is recorded by Eratosthenes of Alexandria and can also be traced in the Old British Chronicles by Gildus Albanius (fifth century), Nennius (ninth century) and Bishop Geoffrey of Monmouth (twelfth century).

Brutus was born and grew up under the yolk of the Greeks; but he distinguished himself so much in various battles that he was given his freedom. So, together with a band of his countrymen, he set sail to find out his fate. The following is an extract from Professor Waddell's *Phoenician Origin of Britons, Scots, and Anglo-Saxons* (translated from the Latin):

The winds continued fair for two days and a night together, when at length they arrived at a certain island called Leogecia which had been formerly wasted by pirates and was then uninhabited.... in it was a desolate city in which they found a temple of Diana and in it a statue of that goddess, which gave answers to those that came to consult her ....Brutus, himself, holding before the altar of the goddess a consecrated vessel filled with wine and the blood of a white hart, prayed:

> *'Goddess of Woods, tremendous in the chase*
> *To the mountain boars and all the savage race!*
> *Wide o'er the ethereal walks extend thy sway,*
> *And o'er the infernal mansions void of day!*
> *Look upon us on earth! unfold our fate,*
> *And say what region is our destined seat?*
> *Where shall we next thy lasting temples raise?*
> *And choirs of virgins celebrate thy praise?'*

After repeating this prayer, he took four turns round the altar, poured the wine into the fire and then laid himself down upon the hart's skin, which he had spread before the altar, where he fell fast asleep. In the night, in his deep sleep, the goddess seemed to appear before him and thus responded:

> *'Brutus! there lies beyond the Gallic bounds*
> *An island which the western sea surrounds,*
> *By giants once possessed; now few remain*
> *To bar thy entrance, or obstruct thy reign.*
> *To reach that happy shore thy sails employ;*
> *There Fate decrees to raise a second Troy,*
> *And found an empire in thy royal line*
> *Which Time shall ne'er destroy, nor bounds confine.'*

Awakened by the vision they set sail again. There follows a lengthy series of adventures until Brutus finally arrived here and sailed up the river Dart to Totnes. This seems to be a harbour for the famous, as it was used by Sir Walter Raleigh and, more recently, has been the location of the Royal Yacht Britannia.

The *Chronicles* tell us that Brutus travelled round the whole of the island in search of a place to build his city. When he came to the river Thames, he found the very spot he had been looking for, and in the course of time the city was built and he called it New Troy. Later, it came to be known as 'Trinovantum'.

Edward the Confessor contributed support to the Brutus legend, in the form of documentary evidence. He speaks of London thus: 'a city founded and built after the likeness of Great Troy.'

When Lludd began his reign in 72 BC, he issued an edict commanding the city to be re-named Llud-din, eventually corrupted into Llud-don, or London! It is said that the sites of London and Wincobank Hill in Sheffield are two of the oldest, continually inhabited sites in Europe. So it is quite feasible to argue that Brutus, although settling near the Thames, joined an already-established colony of people who were, even then, seasoned travellers.

Yet another testimony to the coming of Brutus is given in the vestry of the church of St Peter-upon-Cornhill in London. The relevant passage from a lengthy scroll states that King Lucius reigned in this land after Brute (Brutus). The *British Chronicles* give a complete list of the early kings of Britain - seventy-three, in all, together with the dates and duration of their reigns, the authenticity of which I see no reason to doubt. The first king mentioned is Brutus, with the date of 1103 BC.

The Elizabethan poet Drayton speaks of Brutus's arrival:

> *Isle of Albion highly bless'd*
> *With giants lately stored . . .*
> *Where from the stock of Troy, those puissant*
> *   kings should rise*

Whose conquests from the West, the world should scant suffice.

Spenser, too, in the *Faerie Queen,* refers to 'Noble Britons sprung from Trojans bold'. It would seem perfectly natural for Brutus to be led to a country whose people, like himself, worshipped the Goddess Diana. And the prophecy which the Goddess gave to him has been fulfilled, in that Britain, has, despite many invasions, continued to withstand all attempts to change its age-old values of democracy and freedom.

Our historical records were pushed into a convenient dustbin by pro-Roman minds. Eighteenth-century German scholars declared Brutus and his birth-place, the city of Troy, to be a myth. They even declared that there never had been a city called Troy. It was a 'poet's dream'! This, despite the story of the siege and destruction of the city, related in Homer's *Iliad.* We have to thank Professor Schliemann, who re-established the truth of the matter, by uncovering the ruins of the ancient city of Troy, at Hisserlik in Asia Minor.

There are many mysteries in Britain which are thousands of years old. The turf-cut mazes, known as the 'Walls of Troy', or Troy Town are further pointers to the Trojan colonization. The most interesting ones remaining to us are at Saffron Waldon, where the maze measures 138 by 100 feet, while its paths are about a mile in length; on the Winton (sacred mound) at Winchester, and at Alkborough on the Humber, known as Julian's Bower.

The patterns of these mazes are identical to the ones seen on the old coins of Crete. The well-known Cretan statue of a priestess of the Goddess, holding aloft twin snakes, is very similar to a stone carving of the Romano-Celtic goddess, Verbeia, at Ilkley Church in Yorkshire. She, too, holds twin snakes (often quite erroneously described as *reeds*), and wears the tiered dress of the Cretan figure. There is also an altar to this goddess which once stood near the waters of the river Wharfe, in the same town.

Although similar ideas and methods occur in religious thought which can be continents apart, it is not to be supposed that one is copied from another. The phenomena, known to occultists as Divine Illumination, is well known. At certain times there descends a ray of wisdom which envelops the whole globe and germinates in the subconscious minds of human beings, who then interpret the ray according to their own particular socio-religious culture. Partaking of the wafer and the wine, symbolical of the body and blood of the Christ, is analogical to the ancient Greek Mysteries, where the bread was eaten, to be 'at one' with Demeter, the Earth Mother, and the wine drunk so that the spirit of Dionysus would enter the devotee. There are many such similarities throughout the world at all levels of religious thought.

On 7th June 1976, a 12-inch statue of a stone goddess was discovered among some rocks in the garden of a house at Castleton in Derbyshire. It was identified by an expert of Manchester University as an 'idol', connected with an old religion at the Mam Tor (Mother Mountain), of about 2,500 years ago. She has been described as the goddess 'with a sensuous wink', as one eye is larger than the other. Soon after the statue was found, she was placed in the local church, where, on the day of the annual garlanding ceremony, I happened to see her.

The origins of the Castleton Garland are hidden in pre-history, but it is a surviving form of the 'Green Man', who represents the masculine forces behind nature made manifest in the growth of all vegetation. He is another aspect of the Horned God and is also known as 'Green Jack'. As with the Goddess he has many names according to the locality.

The man who carries the garland on his shoulders is called the 'king' and rides at the head of the procession on its way round the village. The Lady rides behind him and they are followed by the local band, which precedes a group of dancers, the village schoolgirls, dressed in white and carrying posies and coloured streamers.

In early times the 'Lady' was a man dressed in women's clothes, and this is a custom often seen in folk festivals all over Britain not to mention the traditional Dame in pantomime. The reason behind this impersonation goes back a very long way, and is really an 'acting out' of the fact that Divinity is both male and female.

The garland, itself, is a beautiful work of art. It is made of all kinds of flowers which are tied in rows on a bell-shaped structure. A separate conical posy is fitted on the top of the garland and is known as the 'queen'. The whole pyramid of flowers is about three feet high and weighs a hundred pounds. The King is completely hidden within it, the weight being taken by strong leather straps which fit over his shoulders.

The 'queen' posy is taken off during the procession to the church and kept until the end of the ceremony when the king places it on the village War Memorial and the 'Last Post' is sounded.

The tower of the church is decorated with branches of oak, fixed to all the pinnacles, except one. The two riders enter the churchyard alone and proceed to the tower, where a rope is let down and the garland is taken up and placed over the remaining pinnacle, where it stays until the flowers have withered. Now, surely, this last act is one of consummation:the 'female' garland 'mated' with the upstanding pinnacle! When this has been accomplished a great cheer goes up from the watching crowds, and as dusk approaches, the schoolgirls perform dances around the village maypole. And now, with the recovery of the Goddess statue, she takes her place beside her consort, the Green Man, in a village which continues to celebrate the return of life to the earth.

This is only one of many thousands of similar ceremonies perpetuated throughout the country. Most of them celebrate the same thing, namely, commemoration of the forces of life - the Ancient Providence, sometimes Christianized, sometimes in their original forms as the Great Goddess and Her Consort, the Horned God, the oldest deities of Britain.

4 Gerald Brosseau Gardner

Many people assert that modern witchcraft has no connection with the past. They postulate, quite wrongly, that it only came into being through the interest, writings and activities of the late Gerald Brosseau Gardner. Certainly Gerald pioneered the great revival of the Craft, and brought it back into the public eye, but as an *initiated* member of the New Forest coven. There were, there are, and there always will be witches. And. speaking personally, I have letters and contacts that prove the religion of witchcraft has had a continuity that bridged the persecution times and has been practised, in secret right up to the present century.

One of these contacts, who was descended from a witch family in Inverness, had visited Gerald Gardner in the Isle of Man before she wrote to me. And although they did not see eye to eye on many aspects of the Craft, she considered him to be 'of the blood'.

There are many hundreds of similar cases of witch families in the UK and elsewhere. They have handed down the secrets, from generation to generation and the knowledge has *not* been lost.

I consider that Gerald, who did a great deal of the spade-work in bringing a new recognition to witchcraft, deserves a chapter in a book which is devoted to the subject.

An early photograph of Gerald Gardner which he gave to the author. It is signed on the reverse:- "Yours eternally, G. B. Gardner - 'Scire' "

I was introduced to Gerald by my late husband, Arnold Crowther, who, incidentally, introduced Gerald to the late Aleister Crowley on 1st May 1947. A meeting confirmed in Crowley's diary for that year. Crowley was very pleased to see Arnold and Gerald told them that he did not think people were any longer interested in magic. How wrong he was! Especially, in view of the fact that his brilliant, prolific works on the magical arts are in constant demand in the present day.

My husband had known G.B.G., (as Gerald was called by his friends), for some fifteen years before we met in 1956 in a summer show at the Pier Casino, Shanklin, Isle of Wight. In the course of time, knowing my deep interest in the Old Religion, he wrote to Gerald at his Museum of Witchcraft in Castletown, Isle of Man.

Arnold received a reply inviting us both to the island. When we arrived the housekeeper told us that Dr. Gardner was very ill and could see no one. 'Let them come up', called a voice from within. We ascended the stairs quietly and entered his bedroom. Gerald was propped up in bed with huge pillows. 'Come in, come in, grand to see you.' He held out his arms to us, beaming. I looked into a pair of mesmeric blue eyes and felt the warm grip of his hands in mine. 'Darling, do sit down.' His white hair stood up in defiance of brush or comb, a fact which I learned later. A small, goatee beard and a weatherbeaten skin completed the picture.

He told Arnold and me that the housekeeper had wanted our address in order to postpone our visit, but he had pretended that he couldn't find it. I was rather worried at his condition, but he assured me that now Arnold had arrived he would soon recover. He told us that he had been very ill in a hospital in London some years before, when Arnold had visited him. He had laughed so much by the time the visit ended that he had felt a great deal better. Sure enough, two days later, Gerald was up and pottering about the house. Unlike Arnold, I did not meet his lovely wife, Donna, as she had died a few months previously.

That first meeting impressed me very deeply. I can honestly say that I had never met anyone quite like him before. There was a gentleness about him; his voice was soft and his eyes bright and humourous. He loved a good joke and would laugh heartily, banging his fist and saying, 'Damned good!' He enjoyed life in spite of health handicaps and asthma as his constant companion since early youth. A typical Geminian, with his air of restlessness, interest in writing, reading, travelling, and looking after his Museum of Witchcraft. His appearance, too, was Geminian: tall, with long arms and legs, and clever hands. His pet hobby was making all kinds of metal jewellery and magical tools. He was also a good artist, and I own three of his paintings, which now hang in my covenstead.

His fingers were forever pushing through his thick, white hair, or tugging at his beard. Added to his remarkable intelligence was an intangible 'something' which to me linked directly with reincarnation. In Gerald, as in Arnold, could be seen an 'old soul'; someone who had seen many earth lives. This was substantiated by Gerald himself when he told us of an incident that had happened in Crete. This had been preceded by a succession of curious dreams which seemed to be connected with a previous life. In them, he was in charge of the building of a huge wall to keep out invaders. It was a hot country and he 'remembered' seizing all kinds of bronze pots and kettles, in order to make them into spears and other weapons. Now this is strange, as in this life he had made a deep study of the Malayan keris while he was working for the British Government in the Far East and had written a book on the subject, *Keris and other Malay Weapons*. And he had a marvellous collection of daggers and swords from all parts of the world.

On the occasion of the author's marriage to Arnold Crowther (9 November 1960) with special guest, Gerald Gardner (centre). By courtesy of the Daily Express

On the day before he sailed for Cyprus in 1938, he had had quite a different dream. In it there was a man who found that he was unwanted at home, so he retreated into the past, with apparent ease - where he *was* needed.

Arriving in Nicosia he called at the museum and chatted to the Curator, who, knowing of GBG's interest in weapons, asked him if he knew how the ancient Cypriots hafted their swords. The Curator handed Gerald a heavy bronze blade and told him of the many experts who had tried without success to solve the puzzle.

Gerald asked if he might take the blade and the various bits and pieces away with him and think about the problem. The Curator acquiesced and wished him luck. But the following day he had a shock, as Gerald gave him the completed sword! The museum authorities wanted to know how he done it, and Gerald told them that he had given up the analytical approach, and then, suddenly, his hands felt as if they knew how to do it. They tried to take the sword to pieces again, but they couldn't. Indeed, they had to get an axe to split it! Later, Gerald made similar hilts for the British Museum. Could he have been using the skills of a previous existence, when he was a swordmaker in Cyprus?

This adventure was not the only one he experienced in that country. On his return the following year, he was to recognise places hitherto only seen in dreams. One of them was at Kyrenia. It was at the mouth of a river, named Stronglos. He found the site much altered, with the river silted up. Yet, he knew this was where he had kept his ships many hundreds of years before. He *remembered* it, and eventually bought that particular piece of land. (See the fascinating life story: *Gerald Gardner: Witch*, by J.L. Bracelin).

Another strange thing in Gerald's life was how something of great importance always happened to him every nine years.

He had traced this back to childhood, but later happenings included meeting his wife, opening his museum of witchcraft, and being presented at Buckingham Palace.

He confided to Arnold and me in 1963 that the following year would be another 'nine' year, and added, 'I suppose I shall pop off then, as I can't think of any other important thing that could happen to me'. True to his own prediction he passed over on 12 February 1964, eighty years young, on the eve of the old pagan festival of Lupercalia!

It seems that the mysterious cycle is still in effect, as, although GBG is no longer with us, in 1973 *nine* years after his passing, his museum of magic and witchcraft was sold and the contents sent to America!

My late husband and I were the last members of the Craft to see Gerald. We drove him over the Pennines from Sheffield to the Manchester Ship Canal, where he boarded a cargo boat for his long journey to the Lebanon and sunshine. It was pouring with rain as we helped him with his luggage up the steep, iron steps on to the ship. Tears mingled with the raindrops on my face, as we waved him good-bye. I was very upset about him going so far on a boat which had no doctor on board, as he wasn't at all well. I could see no reason for such a long journey, when he could have flown to a warmer clime much more quickly.

Gerald, however, could be very obstinate at times, and was not to be dissuaded. Sad to say, it was his last voyage, as he suffered a slight stroke, and died on board the *Scottish Prince* on his way home to England. A week previously I had been told by a clairvoyant, that an old gentleman friend of mine would die very soon.

I must express my deep gratitude to Gerald Gardner for initiating me in this life into the Hollow Mysteries, and giving, both Arnold and myself, the benefit of his considerable knowledge of witchcraft.

I also had the honour to be crowned by him 'Queen of the Sabbat', which is an old French title for the Maiden, or High Priestess, when she was known as '*La Reine du Sabbat*'.

Gerald was initiated by a hereditary group of witches in the New Forest, some of them known to me. But they believed, as do most pagans, in reincarnation and that Gerald had belonged to the Craft in a previous life. Indeed, his sponsor said to him: 'You are of the blood; you were one of us before; come back to us.'

It was as a member of this coven that Gerald took part in 'Operation Cone of Power'. The year was 1940 and Hitler was busy planning the invasion of Britain. 'Operation Sea-Lion', as it was called, was due to be put into effect in late August or September. On Lammas Eve many covens met in the New Forest to fight Hitler on a psychic level. The following details of this extraordinary ceremony are quoted from *Gerald Gardner: Witch* by Jack Bracelin:

> '*We were taken at night to a place in the Forest, where the Great Circle was erected; and that was done which may not be done except in great emergency. And the great Cone of Power was raised and slowly directed in the general direction of Hitler. The command was given: 'You cannot cross the Sea. You cannot cross the Sea. You cannot come: you cannot come!' Just as, we were told, was done to Napoleon, when he had his army ready to invade England and never came. And, as was done to the Spanish Armada, mighty forces were used, of which I may not speak. Now to do this means using one's life-force; and many of us died a few days after we did this. My asthma, which I had never had since I first went out East, came back badly. We repeated the ritual four times;*

and the Elders said: 'We feel we have stopped him. We must not kill too many of our people. Keep them until we need them.'

Whether you believe in the efficacy of this ritual or not, the facts are that the invasion plans were put off, and Hitler turned his attention to Russia!

Gerald initiated me and I initiated my husband. That is how the Craft is passed on - from man to woman, and from woman to man. Many of the secrets are communicated orally, and are never committed to paper. They are given from mouth to ear, and in no other way. So, although the so-called 'initiation' ceremony has appeared in many occult books, the important magical secrets have not been degraded in this way.

To return for a moment to my witch friend in Inverness. Originally, she had seen me on television while she was staying in Durham, and considered I was worthy to receive the tradition which had been given to her by her grandmother. When I compared the rites she sent to me with those of Gerald Gardner, I found them to be very similar, though not identical. This is as it should be, as different covens have different methods, but the basic essentials are always the same, i.e. the working tools, the eight paths to the centre, and the worship of the God and the Goddess.

My friend sent to me her athame (black-handled knife), which had belonged to her grandmother, together with a peculiarly shaped stone which had adorned their altar. It appeared that her mother had not been interested in witchcraft, so my friend was initiated, in her youth, by her grandmother, who was in her turn brought in by her mother and father. In point of fact, her grandmother had been conceived in the Circle itself. This would make for a very strong and powerful witch. And according to my friend, her grandmother had certainly been.

At the time she wrote to me, this old lady was living with in-laws who were Catholics, and she was soon to go to Spain with them to live there, as she was entirely dependent upon them, owing to her illness. She told me she had destroyed her Book of Shadows, as they were inquisitive people, but knew she had to pass on her knowledge to a suitable person before embarking upon a journey from which she knew she would not return. The belief that a witch must transmit her knowledge to another witch before leaving this Plane is a very ancient idea. There have been many cases of witches being unable to die until this condition has been fulfilled.

This wise old lady's opinion of Gerald Gardner cannot be dismissed in view of the genuine tradition she had inherited. It is a pity that I cannot give her name, but I must uphold the promise I gave to her and the sacred trust she placed in me. As I have already stated, she thought Gerald to be 'of the blood', but that he had evidently altered some of the aspects of the rituals to make them more 'respectable' in the eyes of modern 'civilized' people. This, she declared, was not acceptable in the worship of the Old Gods, where such things as prudery and false modesty had no place.

Yet this criticism is a far cry from the accusations levelled by less learned minds against Gardner in recent years. In the main, I believe they stem from jealousy or envy, as most of the people who made the attacks on his character had never met him! The fact that Gerald left a sizeable fortune, together with property which included the museum on the Isle of Man was enough to start the gossip.

Many writers informed the public that he had made his money out of witchcraft. As it happens, Gardner's parents were business people and well-to-do. His father, William Robert Gardner was of the family of Joseph Gardner & Sons Ltd, Liverpool and London, which was the oldest private company in the timber trade in the Empire. Trading with all parts of the world from 1748 to 1948, they were one of the earliest residential families in Liverpool, going back to one Thomas Gardner a leading burgess, who died in 1604.

Some of Gerald's ancestors became Mayors of Liverpool, and one, Alan Gardner, who joined the Royal Navy in 1755 at the age of thirteen, was commanding his own ship before the age of twenty-five. He fought in the West Indies under Rowe and Rodney and later became a Vice-Admiral. His achievements extended to becoming an MP, and then a peer, Baron Gardner of Uttoxeter. In 1807 he was C-in-C of the Channel Fleet, which did much to deter the invasion of Napoleon.

It can be seen from these facts that Gerald was financially independent. In fact he spent a small fortune in bringing together his vast collection of witchcraft relics and magical paraphernalia, not to mention his wonderful collection of swords and daggers. The only money he received was from his books - the entitlement of any author.

All in all, Gerald's was a very colourful character, kindly, with a great curiosity in people. Of course, everyone has faults, and Gardner was no exception, but on many levels I have yet to meet his equal.

One thing is certain. Many people have found their way to happiness and contentment in the age-old worship of the Old Gods. They have become aware of the latent, psychic capabilities in themselves and others. Once more, they tread the ways of their ancestors, and know their spiritual destiny lies in the stars.

That this is so is due largely to Gerald Gardner: the Mercurial Herald of the Old Religion. And on this one count alone, his actions were completely justified.

5 Initiation

To become a witch you must have a natural inclination to worship the Old Gods. It must be a feeling which springs from the heart and carries you on towards your goal, in exactly the same way it happened to the first witches thousands of years ago.

The approach must be in this manner. Any other attitude, such as vulgar curiosity, a desire for power over others, or the selfish intention of using magic to gain material ends, will only end in failure and disillusion.

The Old Gods are ancient archetypal images of the divine powers behind all Nature. They are the oldest gods known to man. Pictures of them are painted in the dark depths of caverns all over Europe and show the great influence they had, even at the Dawn of Time.

Just because they are so old, is no reason to believe they are in any way 'out of date'. Our ancestors were no fools: their way of life and their culture is gaining more and more respect as the years go by. Continuous discoveries about their skills and beliefs brings growing admiration and amazement.

Their deities were a Mother Goddess and a Horned God, representing the twin forces of life: male and female, light and dark, positive and negative, Sun and Moon, etc. These complementary aspects in nature are fact and cannot be disputed. And, because the Gods are true representations of the divine powers behind all manifestation, they have endured through millennia, and will always endure.

Unlike many other religions, where contact with divinity is sought through prayer and meditation, witchcraft teaches development of the soul through the Eight Paths of the Witches' Wheel. These ways are part of the Western Mystery Tradition.

The West and the East are two very different places. Eastern religions teach their followers to look *within* for enlightenment, and although the West uses this method in meditation, it is only *one* of the Eight Paths. The Western mind looks *outward* and seeks spiritual grace by helping others. Thus, the witches use their powers to help those in sickness of trouble.

The Awakening can begin as an urge which rises from the depths of the soul. A state of boredom or desperation, which every human being comes to at some point of incarnation, can become as a beacon to the spirit.

It is born to the struggling soul and to the complacent alike. Many lives may be endured before it is realized that the true self must take the initiative and begin to fight its own way out of the Cycles of Incarnation, which, without the control of the Higher Self, may continue indefinitely. Once the realisation is born, and the quest begun, the soul is on its way from manhood to godhood.

Regarding the Craft, it is wise to seek initiation from a *genuine* coven. This is not as easy as it sounds, because genuine adherents do not seek converts, and therefore do not advertise for members. They believe that if a person is sincere and determined enough in their desire to belong to the Craft, they will, sooner or later, make contact.

There are, however, various ways of speeding things up a little, such as contributing to one of the privately printed occult magazines, which are usually run by people 'in the know'. Or even placing a small advert in one of these papers. You can also write to the author of a book on the subject, and send the letter via the publishers. It might then be forwarded to a coven in your area, although I must add here that even if this happens, and you are invited to meet someone from a coven, it would not be indicative of entry.

There are certain conditions which have to be fulfilled, such as blending in with the personalities of the members, having read widely on the subject, a willingness to submit to a waiting period, usually a year and a day, among others. Yet these conditions are valid ones; you cannot expect to be accepted quickly, but you will know that the witches you meet have undergone similar obstacles themselves.

The ways of the witches are those of caution, especially where strangers are concerned. After all, who would admit a stranger to their home without an introduction, let alone to a temple of the Mysteries.

Care must be taken, too, in finding a coven which is in close rapport with your own life-style, culture and character. But, once contact is made, there is hope in finding a group where conditions, on both sides, can be fulfilled.

Although some covens wear robes, the traditional way of working in the Circle, is to be sky-clad, or naked. When you are brought into the Craft, you enter as you were born, without clothes or ties of any kind. The first initiation is virtually an introduction to a new way of life. You are made a 'Child of the Goddess'; you are shown the tools of the Craft; told the ways of working magic, and made to swear an oath to keep the secrets of the Art. This is called the First Degree.

The Second Degree is the initiation proper. This involves the concept of symbolic death and symbolic resurrection, when you are re-born with new knowledge and a new magical personality. A new name (of your own choice) is given to you which represents the transformation, and by which, henceforth, you will be known when in the Circle.

The drama of this mystery play implants its ideas firmly in the subconscious mind of the adherent, and the mystery, which is enacted on the material plane, sets the seal on the future.

It is not to be supposed that by initiation and teaching you will automatically be 're-born'. A way will be shown, and knowledge imparted, yet the journey is always alone and the true will tested to the very brink of breaking point.

In a sense, when initiation takes place it is very much like daring Fate to do its worst. One has taken a stand: 'I announce to all creation that I will endure to progress.'

In witchcraft the soul develops a deeper understanding of *being*. This entails practice, which is why the Craft has grades of advancement. The highest grade is the consummation of the mysteries, where ritual yields to what is termed, 'The Secret of the Silver Wheel'.

There is also the imparting of certain 'secret' words, which, in themselves, convey very little, but their secret intention *is* important and gently 'nudges' the aspirant onward.

The symbol of the Craft is the pentagram or five-pointed star. Of very ancient origin and used in most esoteric societies, it is a perfect geometric shape and contains many meanings. Principally, the five points represent the Four Elements (Earth, Water, Air and Fire), plus Spirit (Mind ruling over Matter), and the five major planets, Saturn, Jupiter, Mars, Venus and Mercury. An upward pointing triangle above the pentagram is peculiar to the Craft. It symbolizes the Sun and the Moon (male and female), the twin forces of life, with

Divinity as the top-most point from whom everything issues. This is the goal of the initiate: to be a fully individualized being who has mastered the elements in Nature and within the self, and has become a Star of the Microcosm in touch with the Macrocosm.

It will now be understood that the physical vehicle is the house of the soul, and it is in this unique structure that true initiation is enacted. The soul enters the body to undergo the experience of terrestrial life and when the Gate of the Mysteries swings back, the soul awakes and the consciousness is flooded with memories of the past, and knowledge of its real destiny.

Not all of the Craft's teachings can be disclosed here. The real reason for secrecy lies in the concept of the word *mystery*. For this word suggests to the mind something 'out of the ordinary'; something which is unknown, and therefore, fascinating. This, in turn, awakens the mind to the idea of strange experiences, and prepares it for new understanding.

The aim of ritual is to induce the state of rapture or ecstasy. The shifting of the centre of consciousness is the goal. This ecstasy is not the same a sexual fulfilment. It is a thing of the spirit and not easily explained in words. There are many ways in which this condition can be captured, such as the use of music, dancing, and the utterance of calls or chants. These will be examined in later chapters.

It is very necessary to cultivate, or re-awaken the spirit of youth, to have a childlike, not childish, approach to these methods, because without it any progress (other than intellectual) will be almost impossible to achieve.

The Christian Church has always frowned upon and deliberately repressed these fundamental expressions of joy; they are considered undignified and unseemly, etc. There has been a restricting of man's spirit for the worst possible reasons. The only existence of which he is now aware is that of ordinary, mundane living. It is a very necessary thing for people to free themselves from the yoke of habit. That is why a change of scenery and occupation is vital.

Desperation has given the modern drug craze a recognition it does not deserve. It can be argued that some drugs *do* raise the consciousness to a more spiritual level. Yet, it is an artificial stimulation which requires repeated induction. This, in turn, leads naturally to a stage when the person becomes well and truly 'hooked'. It is true that in ancient times certain drugs were used for transcendental purposes, but these were kept secret, and their uses given only to the wisest among the priesthood.

Most medicines are poisons and have to be administered in the correct quantity, and only for a specific period. How much more dangerous is the use of drugs which affect the brain cells! We yet know so little about the brain and its capabilities, which only now, in the present day, are being explored. The methods which are taught in the Old Religion are completely natural, and the resulting extension of consciousness, although attained more slowly, is one which allows *continuation* of growth and enlightenment.

There is no longer any law to forbid you from becoming a pagan, if this is your wish. The Universal Declaration of Human Rights, to which Britain has added her signature, gives you this freedom of choice. As published by the United Nations, Article No. 18, states: 'Everyone has the right to freedom of thought, conscience and religion; this right includes freedom to change his religion or belief, and freedom, either alone or in community with others and in public or private, to manifest his religion or belief in teaching, practice, worship and observance'.

Although, belonging to a genuine group is obviously advantageous, there is nothing to stop you from practising on your own, or with your partner. Witches who are members of a coven always have a place of worship in their own homes. This is essential, as you do not switch off your allegiance at the end of a meeting. It is a part of your life whatever you are doing, and wherever you happen to be. It is also helpful during the period of searching for a suitable coven. You can put forth the thought and pray to be guided in the right direction.

It may be that you are not free to join a coven, for whatever reasons. Should this be so, you will need to know the basic necessities. Therefore, I am going to explain how to form a Magic Circle, what tools you require, and the attributes of the Four Elements.

Casting the Circle

The circle can be made in several ways as long as it is nine feet in diameter. Nine is the number of the Moon and the circle is a symbol of the Womb of the Goddess. It can be drawn in chalk on a special carpet, which is used only for the rituals; or marked with a white cord, perhaps a more convenient method. Once you have the correct length, it can be put down anywhere. This is achieved by having a piece of cord just over four-and-a-half feet long, in which a loop is made at one end. In olden times, the witch would place the loop round her athame (magical knife), and stick it into the ground. Then, by fastening a piece of chalk on the other end, she would trace the circle on the floor, starting in the East and working 'deosil' or clockwise round the room until she again reached the East, which gives a circle of the proper dimensions.

It is necessary to have a compass to ascertain the alignments correctly, as the altar must always face North. This is considered to be the right place because the magnetic currents flow from North to South. The witches of old said that the North was the Home of the Gods; they probably felt these currents but had a different way of expressing the same thing.

Unlike the ritual magician's circle, which is there to keep elementals and hostile forces at bay, the witches' circle is erected to contain the magical power raised within it. A sacred place, which lies 'between the worlds', both spiritual and material.

The circle is also a symbol of infinity - without beginning or ending.

Your altar can be a small table or chest; if the latter, you can keep your magical equipment inside it. If you do use a chest, remember to take out everything you need before using it as an altar. Otherwise, it means removing everything off it in order to get at something you have forgotten.

You will require five or six candlesticks. One or two for the altar, and four for the Gates of the Circle; East, South, West and North. These latter are placed just outside the circumference. What you are doing is creating a miniature cosmos in which you are the ruler.

Statues, or pictures of the God and the Goddess, can be placed upon the altar, or, alternatively, symbols such as a holed stone and a phallic-shaped one may be used, as long as their presence is associated with divine duality.

A container filled with sand or earth is necessary for the burning of incense in the form of joss-sticks. Or you may prefer an actual thurible, or censer. If the latter, you will have to purchase charcoal and incense in crystal form. Then, it is a matter of lighting the charcoal and sprinkling the crystals upon it.

Sweet-smelling incense purifies the air and also helps in elevating the mind to the things of the spirit. As the smoke rises it represents your thoughts and prayers rising to the Gods.

A bowl of water and a container of salt are needed for consecrating both the circle and yourself. Also, a sprinkler, which can be a small bunch of herbs tied together.

A sweet-toned bell should also be present, to be struck when invoking the Kings of the Elements. Sometimes a horn is used for this purpose, but it is entirely a matter of preference.

The Magical Tools

The most important of the magical tools is the black-handled knife, or athame (pronounced ath-ay-me). It is virtually an extension of the operator's will and determination: to invoke the Elemental Lords at the four quarters, to send forth the power of the witch in the direction required, and to banish and cleanse the working area.

During the persecutions, the black handle helped to differentiate it from the white-handled knife, when all instruments used in the Art had to be ordinary household utensils, or appear to be! The knife with the white handle was used solely to carve or cut anything of a practical nature within the circle.

The origins of the athame go back a very long way. An old Irish ballad relates the story of a young woman who disappeared and was presumed dead. But a year later she was seen sitting on a fairy mound, rocking her fairy baby and singing a lullaby. Between her words, she gave instructions to her real husband on how she could be rescued. 'To come with a wax candle in the palm of his hand and to quickly bring a *black-handled knife*, and strike the first horse going through the gap into the hillock. Then, pluck the herb in the doorway of the fairy fort. If he failed, she would have to stay and become the queen of the fairies.'

This story shows the magical qualities of the knife which links with success, and victory over opposition. When I was initiated, Gerald Gardner gave me a silver-handled knife. He assured me it would 'do the job', but seemed convinced that one which was meant for me would, in time, make its appearance. It did! As stated previously, the Scottish witch sent me her grandmother's knife which had the traditional black handle.

There could be a link between the athame, and the skean-dhu, which is worn in the stocking of a Scottish Highlander. My husband, whose mother was a MacFarlane, often wore the kilt when performing his stage and cabaret act. He told me that skean-dhu means 'black knife'.

The athame is usually about nine inches long. One found in the grave of a priestess in Norway (a copy of which is in my possession) measures the same length. It has the same symbols engraved on the handle as the ones used in the present day.

As you do not command the Gods to attend your circle, during invocations and prayers, the athame is relinquished in favour of the Wand. This is a symbol of the energy and life-force within you and is also the universal Phallus of Life. It is the Magic Wand of world-wide fame. Medieval magicians have always used this tool in their magical operations, and even stage magicians retain the Magic Wand to make things appear or disappear.

Some wands are made of ivory or ebony and are beautifully carved; but an effective one can be cut with your white-handled knife from a hazel tree, when the Moon is waxing or full. It should be cut on a Wednesday; both tree and day belonging to Mercury. You can then trim and carve it according to your own personal taste, perhaps giving it a phallic tip. Another artefact with the same connotations is the Riding Pole (see Chapter 11).

The next implement to obtain is a cauldron. But, as they are rather large in comparison to the other tools, some witches use a black bowl, or horned cup, upon the altar. The cauldron, when filled with water, is an excellent instrument for the art of scrying, or as a container for a small fire in the circle. The safest way to achieve this is to place some coils of asbestos twine in a round tin, upon which you pour a small quantity of methylated spirit. Put the tin in the cauldron and light the methylated spirit which gives you a bright flame with practically no smell. The fire is necessary when celebrating one of the ancient Fire Festivals of the witches' year. If you can purchase a gypsy-pot, this is ideal for the circle as they are quite small, though comparatively rare these days.

The Celtic Moon Goddess was associated with a magic cauldron which the goddess brewed for a year and a day. At the end of that time, there flew out three drops of the Grace of Inspiration. The goddess, Cerridwen, gives the gifts of poetry, inspiration and wisdom to her devotees: the ancient Druids' Mistress of Art. The three legs of the cauldron refer to the three phases of the Moon, and the three aspects of the Goddess - Maiden, Mother and Crone. Added to which, as a hollow vessel it is a feminine symbol.

The Pentacle is a round or square piece of metal, or even a large, flat stone with a smooth surface. If the latter, the signs can be painted on it in red. A coven pentacle has all the occult symbolism of the Craft engraved on its surface, but as some of these connect with the Three Grades of Initiation it is more sensible to omit them until you are actually working within a coven.

Use instead the Crowned Pentagram, which represents the goal, and any symbols which are meaningful to yourself such as the waxing and waning Moon drawn back to back, or perhaps your own name written in one of the magical alphabets.

The five-pointed star looks like a man standing with his arms and legs apart, and surrounded by a circle depicts man (or woman) working magic. These symbols etched upon the pentacle, represent man, the Magician!

The last essential article you will need is the Cord. The colour of the cord is usually red but it can be a combination of three strands, red, white and blue, plaited together. These being the colours of the three aspects of the Goddess, Virgin, Mother and Crone. Its place in magical workings will be explained in the next chapter. It can be worn round the leg during a ritual, thus absorbing your own vibrations and aura. This cord is the origin of the witches' Garter, considered to denote high rank in the Craft. Today a high priestess usually wears one on her thigh, made of velvet or snakeskin. Anyone who has studied the subject of witchcraft will know of the story about King Edward III, who picked up a lady's garter when she dropped it during a ball. The King did a most unusual thing, placing it upon his own leg with the words 'Honi soit qui mal y pense' (Evil be to him who evil thinks). Now, if it had been an ordinary piece of frippery, it seems highly unlikely that the King would have made such a gesture.

Dr Margaret Murray seemed convinced it was a ritual garter, and the king was a Plantagenet (the name is derived from the broom plant, Planta genista), whose family are said to have held a deep allegiance to the Old Religion. Be that as it may, from that single incident he founded the Most Noble Order of the Garter with a membership of twenty-six knights. Two thirteens are twenty-six! But the significances do not end there. The King built what became known as the Devil's

Tower at Windsor Castle, and upon the very early robes of a knight of this Order, were powdered one hundred and sixty-eight garters, plus the one worn on the leg - 169, or thirteen times thirteen!

There are quite a few medieval paintings of witches that show them wearing the garter, and a cave painting in Cogul, Spain, depicts a man whose only adornment is a pair of garters! He is standing in the centre of a circle of women and it is quite obvious that the garters are of ritual significance.

The cord was used by witches when they sold winds to the sailors. They would sell one with several knots tied in it, and when the sailor untied a knot, a fresh breeze would spring up. The more knots he untied, the greater the wind would become.

The art of knots is a very ancient art. The twining and interlacing was a way of warding off the Evil Eye. The idea was to avert and mislead the eye of any malevolent person by the tracing of knots. The beautiful designs of Celtic art display this form of magic very expressively.

The cord describes the connection between spirit and matter, godhead and man; the ever-present link, inter-penetrating and eternal. It also conjoins the four points of the compass, the four elements, and the binding of the sigils and tools of the Art. Also, it is utilized during the swearing of the oath of allegiance at initiation.

The Four Elements

The athame, rod, cup and pentacle, represent the four elements, Air, Fire, Water and Earth. In the Craft, the intelligences behind the elements are called the 'Lords of the Outer Spaces', or the 'Kings of the Elements'. All religions recognize them under different names, the Christians knowing them as the Archangels Raphael, Michael, Gabriel and Auriel.

Progressing clockwise round the Circle, we begin in the East with Air. Many witches use the Greek Hermes, or the Roman Mercury, in identifying the Lord of Air - the Messenger of the Gods. With winged cap and feet, he darts here and there, communicating between Inner and Outer levels of existence. His caduceus, with its twining serpents, is the Medical profession's emblem, because Mercury is the divine healer. He can also be seen portrayed on the crest of the Royal Corp of Signals, as the medium through which signals are communicated and where he is affectionately known as 'Jimmy'.

There is a statue of Mercury on the top of the *Sheffield Star* newspaper building, standing for the controller of the written word. The Mind is the territory of Mercury which includes the gift of speech - which is carried by Air - the gas in which we live.

The athame links with this element, as it stabs the Air and conveys our magical intent from Outer to Inner levels. The Sun rises in the East, and typifies the dawning of our Inner Light.

At the next Gate of the Circle, that of the South, we encounter the element of Fire, which links with the Magic Wand. We receive this masculine energy in a physical form from the Sun; and the human being, as a miniature cosmos, has its counterpart in the heart, the source of bodily life.

The Wand symbolizes the Power of the Horned God - the Phallic Power of Regeneration. In olden times, it was the meaning behind the stone-pillar and the maypole, the power of Green Jack.

Fire is the most mysterious of the elements. It consumes, yet cannot itself be consumed. It remains pure and inviolate. We may bring it into our lives through friction, which is how early man discovered it, but we can imagine the accidents which occurred before he learned how to control it. He eventually did so by use of a rod or *wand* and could carry it safely from place to place.

Michael, the Leader of the Heavenly Hosts, is the Lord of Fire. He is depicted suppressing evil in the shape of a monster: Light overcoming Darkness.

Care must be taken when using our own power and energy in magic. We should engage our gears and build our 'batteries' slowly with perfect control, because without this control things could easily backfire. Michael can be invoked to heal diseases, the wand becoming a laser beam, in work of this kind.

Some people have had the experience of Divine Illumination, which comes to them as a blinding flash. Truly, this can happen. We humans, in contrast to the Divine Light, live as moles, in darkness. And yet, a tiny spark of that brightness dwells within us. The realisation of this was shown in all ancient temples of occultism in the words: 'Know thyself'.

Progressing round the Circle, we come to Water at the Western Gate. Its equivalent in material terms is the Cauldron, or Horned Cup. We have a very close relationship with this element as it was with us before we were born, when it rocked us in our mother's womb. Also, most of our bodies are made up of water.

It is a feminine element, with the Moon as its ruler. Although the witches worship the Moon Goddess, they do not worship the Moon itself, but the unseen powers which control its actions, and through which it manifests itself.

The fluctuations of the tides is governed by the Moon. The 'Moistener' also regulates the menstrual cycle in women - 'mens' means Moon or Moon-blood - and also rules the pearly-white seminal fluid in men.

The orb is thought to control tides on the Inner levels of Birth and Death, as ruler of the Astral Plane. At physical death the soul passes through the Western Gate into the arms of Gabriel (Jav-ree-el), the life bearer. It was this archangel who came to Mary at the time of her conception. Gabriel rules the Waters of Life, empowered by Love and Compassion. The cup of good cheer is passed round the circle at the end of a meeting, when we drink to one another and create a bond of love and good fellowship.

The Goddess herself says: 'By nought but Love may I be known'. This is not so much a physical love as a spiritual one: love, in its highest context, a thing quite apart from human passion. It is said that for an advanced soul to reincarnate, it is necessary for its would-be parents to know and love each other in the deepest sense of the word. The union of two such minds can open the Gateway, pure enough for an 'old' soul, or teacher, to obtain re-birth.

Water is the element of the emotions, which, if allowed, would dominate our lives. Animals respond to the ebb and flow of the Moon's call and have regular mating seasons. Experiments on oysters show that they open their shells to feed at high tide. And, when removed to an underground chamber, miles away from the sea, they adjust their feeding time-table to coincide with the time the Moon is overhead. This suggests that the Moon rules the minds of animals, but humans, at a higher level of development, are not subject to this compulsion, because their souls are able to contact spiritual realms beyond the Astral.

The Astral tides react to the Moon's pull in the same way as the tides of the sea, bringing souls to birth on an incoming 'tide', and taking them away at physical death. The plasticity of this Plane creates whatever scenes the soul wishes to project around itself when it has left the body, until this palls, and soul slips into a higher dimension of Being. The Astral Plane is the one upon which magic is projected, and, as it is the Inner equivalent of Water, it is likewise pliable and easily moulded to the operator's will. Finer elements, such as Air and Fire, also have their Inner, spiritual levels; these align with the Manasic (Mental) and Buddhic (Masterhood) respectively.

The 'message' of the Cup or Cauldron, in which we gaze at the glittering water, the element of clairvoyance, tells us to cultivate compassion, care and love for one another.

The element at the North point of the Circle is Earth, and naturally equates with the Pentacle or Stone. Earth is our home while we are in the physical body and is our Mother, the bounteous giver of life and sustenance. The altar, as well as the element, is the material basis and foundation upon which we rest our magical implements, and should be reverenced as much, if not more, than our working tools. Facing the magnetic North, the altar is the focal point of all our prayers, invocations and mental prowess.

Although the modern world is becoming more and more aware of the need to preserve and recognize Mother Earth, the Ancients gave her a natural love which came from the heart. They knew, instinctively, the necessity of acknowledging the Mother's gifts in the form of libations poured back into the soil. Sheaves of corn were also returned to her, and the Corn Dolly was made with the last sheaves to be reaped. It was then hung up in barn or cottage in honour of the Goddess. This ancient craft is still preserved, with all kinds of symbols and figures being made in the same manner.

The great Fertility Festivals were held at various times of the year to achieve a rapport with the life of Mother Nature. Echoing and acting out her annual drama of conception, birth, death and re-birth. They felt it was necessary to give their love to all vegetation which appeared with bright green shoots from the darkness of the earth, and that everything grew better and stronger, because of their concern.

Recently, scientific experiments have found this to be so. Plants living close to the house and receiving loving care *do* grow bigger and better than those which grow alone. People often talk to their plants and flowers and a recent report on television showed a machine which can tune in to the language of plants! A peculiar whistling sound issues from the machine when it is attached to them, and, according to the inventor, was answering the questions of the reporter!

It must be realized that the earth is a living entity in her own right and has just past middle age. She is just as much alive as the electrons in an atom, or the corpuscles in human blood.

Auriel is the ruler of Earth element. Usually pictured as standing between fields of gold and green, with mountains rising behind him and rivers flowing beneath his feet. The Sun rises above his head in an 'auriel' of flame.

We, too, must stand firmly upon the earth, with feet apart and arms raised to the stars in the position of the Pentagram. The lesson to be learned from earth is to grow and flower into fully individualized beings, so that the fruits of this incarnation may be gathered and enjoyed in our next stage of existence.

Although the Archangels are not strictly recognized within the Craft, I have included them because they actually pre-date the Christian era, and have been known to practitioners of magic throughout recorded time.

It is equally acceptable to visualize the elements in their natural forms. But contact must be made with their essences at the time of invoking them at the four Gates.

For example, Air may be felt as a breeze, blowing through your hair; feeling it in your breath as it delivers your invocation, or in picturing clouds racing across the sky. Fire, imagined as a blazing bonfire, the Sun in its splendour, or even the flame of a candle. At the West, feel raindrops falling on your upturned face; see a clear, bubbling stream, or the majesty of the sea, with foam-topped, breaking waves. And, finally, the earth can be conjured up as a grove of trees, fields or golden corn, or blue mountains raising their peaks to the sky.

6 Making Magic

Presuming you have all the essentials gathered together, and you are now ready to tread the Path of Magic, read on!

First, you must consecrate all your magical paraphernalia, and to do this you must begin by consecrating the Circle and the altar. It will be taken as read that once everything has been purified and dedicated, your tools of magic should be kept apart from ordinary, everyday things. They should be wrapped in silk or black velvet and put away in a special place.

With regard to your athame, this should be kept close to your person for a time, to ensure it becomes part of you and carries your particular vibrations.

An important item is your book of words. You will collect more and more rituals, spells, poetry and invocations as you progress. Start with a large exercise book in which to incorporate your writings. This is called the Book of Shadows, as it is but a pale shadow of Inner spiritual realities. It can be bound in felt material with the cover embroidered with silks or coloured stones in a way that is pleasing to you. Sometimes pictures of the God and Goddess are pasted on the front. It is possible to fabricate a small stand for it, thus leaving your hands free when you are in the Circle.

This initial ceremony should be performed naked as it is a form of initiation. If female, the wearing of a necklace is essential; this being an ancient symbol of the Goddess. Most ancient statues depict her wearing one - in fact, very little else! At Ephesus, she displays a necklace of acorns, a symbol of fertility. I own a very old statue of the Goddess, adorned with a head-dress and a necklace of large stones. On her knees sits the divine child, Horus, as though she is presenting him to the people.

The necklace has to be made of fairly large beads and lie round the base of the neck, so that it looks like a circle. An ideal necklace can be made from witch-stones. These are, in fact, fossilized sponges, millions of years old. They are perfectly round, quite small, with a natural perforation through them. Often white and faintly glittering, like the Moon, their mistress. They can be found on some parts of the seashore and also in quarries. The museum at Whitby has a necklace of them which they call 'the oldest necklace in the world' - most probably true! I collected a number of them on the beach at Brighton and was lucky enough to find a small heart-shaped stone to act as a fastener. These *Porosphaera globularis* (their correct name), have always been considered to be lucky, primarily because of their female shape and immense age.

Gather everything within the Circle; light the altar candles, the incense, and the candles at the four quarters. These latter may be dedicated lastly, when you can bring them into the Circle; re-draw it, consecrate them; re-place them, and again draw the Circle.

Now say a prayer concerning your intention to the Old Ones, and, whether you are male or female, remember you have aspects of both God and Goddess within you.

Rise, and holding your athame, approach the East to perform the cleansing of the Circle. This must be done every time you work a ritual. Use the Banishing Pentagram (see illustration opposite), and say: '*I cleanse and purify this dedicated place; let all adverse influences depart, depart, depart!*' With the last words, stab your athame through the centre of the star with fierce intent. Moving deosil or sun-wise, repeat at the South, West and North, returning to the East.

The Circle is cast by raising your athame, bringing it down, and tracing a duplicate of the material one with the point of the blade. Again, deosil. When the Circle is completed, lift up the knife and bring the arm back to the body. Perform these actions as if you were actually drawing a circle, seeing a line of blue flame following the point of the athame. It is this Astral circle, which is the most important, the one on the floor acting as a guide on the physical Plane.

Invoking Pentagram

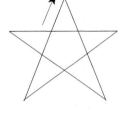

Banishing Pentagram

Take up the bowl of water, saying: '*O! thou creature of water, thee do I purify to my purpose* (tip some salt into the water), *by this salt of earth, be thou truly cleansed. So Mote It Be!*'

Pick up the sprinkler and asperge the Circle. Always begin and end at the East. Next take up the incense and make the round, and say: '*I purify thee O! Circle, to be a fit place for the Gods to enter, and to contain the power which will be raised within thee*'.

To invoke the Kings of the Elements, sound bell or horn, saying: '*I summon, stir, and call ye up, ye Mighty Ones of the East, to aid me and to guard the Circle.*' Draw the Invoking Pentagram with your athame and repeat at the South, West and North, changing the appropriate word, of course. When you sound the instrument, try to imagine the note reverberating on the Astral Plane before you speak.

Approach the altar and sprinkle and cense it with the words: '*I consecrate this altar, that it may be a holy and pleasing Aula to the Gods. Bless this surface and solid foundation; the focus for my worship and work.*'

Touch your forehead, breasts and genitals with a drop of perfumed oil, and say: '*I consecrate this body to be a vehicle for my will; to be at all times subservient to my spirit. I herewith dedicate myself to the Great Goddess and the Horned God. And give my solemn oath that I (name) will follow the Green Way as a true Pagan.*'

Here a token of some kind should be presented and placed upon the altar; later to be put in a little box and kept within, or near the Circle. It could be lock of your hair, an amber bead, or a written representation of your aspirations. Perhaps all three!

After a few moments in meditation, take up the Wand, hold it upright, and recite the following:

> *Enter I, the Circle old,*
> *With heart of love and courage bold.*
>
> *God and Goddess, hear my call,*
> *Guardians of the witches all.*
>
> *Take my token, take my love,*
> *Given Ye, all else to prove.*

As the Mill, around I tread,
guide me in my way ahead.

Forge my spirit, keen and bright,
Leading me into the light.

Spells and symbols, thought and deed,
Prompted by the Wiccan Rede.

Green is the Goddess; Green is the God;
I praise Thee with this flaming Rod.

Then circumambulate the circle to this chant:

I-o-evoe-ee; An and Al I call to Thee;
I-o-evoe-ee; send Thy blessings down on me.

Repeat this as many times as you wish. You will find it becomes hypnotic and will give you a feeling of elation. Begin with a slow walk and gradually build into a quick trot.

When ready, stop suddenly in front of the altar, holding the Wand high. Bow to the altar and rest.

The next step is the consecration of everything on the altar. Each article must be purified separately. The following words are an example, but you may use your own. The Gods have many names, according to country and locality. I have incorporated two of the oldest names used in Britain, but you may choose the ones which appeal to you.

'O! *Ancient Ones; Al and An; in Thy names I consecrate and purify this* ------(name of implement), *that it may be used in Wisdom and Love.*' (Sprinkle and cense it).

When all is accomplished, sit as a witch, i.e. cross-legged, on the floor, and enjoy your surroundings. The Circle will soon take on a cosy, out-of-time atmosphere, quite unlike any other. Especially, if you use it constantly.

You may wish to have a small drink of wine to toast the Gods, and although this ceremony is usually confined to the closing of a ritual, there is nothing against refreshing yourself between the stages of a rite. The wine will warm you and help to alleviate any drowsiness, because, at the beginning of Craft workings, you will be using parts of your mind and awakening centres in your body to which you are unaccustomed. After a while, it will become as second nature, but do not overdo things at first.

The following consecration was given to me by Gerald Gardner, and as it has appeared in print many times before, I see no reason for omitting it here.

Stand before the altar and raise your athame over the cup of wine, saying: *'As the athame is the male, so the Cup is the female, and conjoined they bring blessedness.'*

Slowly lower the tip of the blade into the wine, then raise the knife and lay it back upon the altar. If you have a partner, the female sits upon the altar, holding up her athame. The male kneels before her and adores. He then takes up the Cup, and *she* performs the blessing.

Lift up the Cup and say: *'To the Old Ones! Merry Meet and Merry Part and Merry Meet again!'*

Take a drink of the wine with the words: *'Flags! Flax! Fodder and Frig!'* This is an old blessing which means, Shelter, Clothes, Food and Love - the Four F's! And if you follow the God and Goddess, you will find that you always have enough to make your way in life. As the saying goes: 'The Old Ones never let you starve'. And I have found this to be so.

It is understood that you do not break the Circle by stepping out of it once it has been cast. So, at the end of the ritual, lift up your athame, step to the East and draw the Banishing Pentagram with these words: '*Ye Guardians of the East; I thank ye for attending. Hail and Farewell!*' Continue round the Circle. Never omit the dismissal as the initial 'call' is always heard. In actual fact, it is *we* who attend and depart, as the Gods and Guardians are ever present. We are on the outside of inside, or the other side of the looking-glass; the idea portrayed so vividly in the works of Lewis Carroll. If someone else wishes to worship in the circle with you, it is understood that they can also initiate themselves by the above dedication.

Spells

Magic is made in the mind, but it must be brought into material form. That is why the witch employs cords, candles, talismans and also spells. This really means spelling the wish out in the form of words. Make it into a simple rhyming couplet to recite while you are concentrating, such as, '*Betty will be well a-soon, God and Goddess grant this boon*'. As they are easy to remember, the words seem to say themselves; and you can keep you mind on the object of the exercise.

But bear in mind the Wiccan Rede, or Witches' Creed:

> *Eight words the Wiccan Rede fulfil:*
> *An it harm none, do what ye will!*

Therefore, be very sure that the magic you perform, will not, in any way, harm any person, even indirectly. The approach should be positive. Any negative command is self-defeating. It is also dangerous and very foolish because you are inviting the wrath of the Gods by breaking your oath.

The Waning Moon can be utilized for getting rid of unhealthy vibrations or any imperfections in yourself. Personally, I find the Dark of the Moon an excellent time for divining and clairvoyance, perhaps because this aspect connects with the hidden, mysterious Crone, or Wise One.

Once you start upon the path of witchcraft, there will always be people who will ask you what it is all about. In spite of their questions, tell them nothing. Otherwise, your work will not come to fruition. This is part of the esoteric teachings described in the Four Powers of the Magus. A time-honoured maxim, it embraces the whole idea behind magic in the words 'to know, to dare, to will and to be silent'. The last instruction is one of the hardest to achieve, especially when you begin to get results from your work. There is a strong impulse to tell someone about it. Nevertheless, do your utmost to keep your own council. I think it will be easier for witches born under Capricornus, Taurus or Scorpio to do this, as they are usually reserved and cautious by nature.

However, if you *are* questioned, think immediately of the Sphinx, the silent watcher of the desert, retaining secrets of the past. Gerald Gardner would always say of inquisitive folk; 'there's no harm in *asking*', which means he had no intention of telling them things that were none of their business.

Times for working are discussed in the next chapter, but witches always meet at the Full Moon, the time of maximum lunar power. As the old rhyme tells us:

> *Pray to the Moon when she is round,*
> *Luck with you will then abound.*
> *What you seek for shall be found,*
> *On the sea or solid ground.*

A Candle Spell

Select a candle of the colour appropriate to your wish. A list of colours and their influences are included in the Planetary Rituals. With a little perfumed oil, magnetize the candle. This is done by stroking it with the oil, from the centre to the top, and from the centre to the bottom. This also helps to impregnate the candle with your own aura. Say:

> *Upon this candle I will write,*
> *What I require of Thee tonight.*
> *May the runes of magic flow;*
> *By mind and spell and flame aglow.*
> *I trust that Thou wilt grant this boon;*
> *O! lovely Goddess of the Moon.*

Take up your white-handled knife and carve your wish upon the wax. Start at the top of the candle and gradually work your way round and down towards the bottom. You can use one of the magical alphabets, such as the Theban. This one is popular among witches. Writing in a strange language helps you to concentrate deeply and your intent will be more effective. However, ordinary writing will do until you master the former.

Light the candle and place it upon the altar. It should be allowed to burn out, so when you leave the Circle put it into the cauldron, or some other safe receptacle.

All spells should be preceded by a circle dance while chanting a rhyme which encompasses your wishes in the manner described previously. This action raises the power which comes from the body in the form of energy. When a full coven performs The Mill, great power is raised. It rises from the dancers to a point above the Circle; hence it is known as the Cone of Power. Nevertheless, an adequate amount can be achieved alone if you follow the ways described in the chapter on The Dance.

This particular spell came through me when I was in trance, back in the sixties. We found that it worked; so my husband wrote the above verse to accompany it. Subsequently I read a bowdlerized version of this rhyme in an American book on witchcraft. It was described as an 'Ancient Runic Spell' which had been handed down by *word of mouth* from generations of witch families! The verse was definitely *not* ancient, and there was no explanation of how to perform the spell, which is why I have included it here, together with its true origin!

A Corð Spell

Obtain a number of different coloured cords, roughly, twelve inches in length. The colours are used in the same way as those of the candles.

Select a cord and purify it by passing it through the incense. Holding it between your hands, show it to the four quarters, then return to the altar and announce your intent. The more enthusiasm you can raise, the more likely the result. Keep concentrating and slowly twist the cord around your own *ritual* cord, which, it is assumed, has spent some time tied round your left leg, just above the knee.

The binding of the two cords together will enforce your will. Hold up the twisted cord and say: '*I bind the cords, I bind the spell; in numbers odd, it augurs well!*'

Now, separate the cords and put the ritual one aside. Then, slowly and deliberately, tie three, seven or nine knots in the working cord. These numbers are included in many Craft rituals as it is said that odd numbers are pleasing to the Gods.

As you tie the knots, recite your intent in a simple rhyme, then take the knotted cord and present it at the Four Gates with the words: '*The Air will carry it* (whirl the cord around your head); *The Fire will marry it; the Water will bear it; the Earth will wear it! So mote it be!'*

If the wish is for yourself, keep the cord upon your person for seven days. If it is for another, put it away in some secret place. When the magic has been wrought, retain the cord for nine moons then dispose of it by burning it in the cauldron fire. *It must not be used again.*

A Water Spell

This is a spell which links with any emotional matter: love, friendship, marriage, etc. You must obtain a photograph of the person you wish to help, and this should be laid upon the pentacle.

Fill the cauldron with water and place it upon the altar. Add a little salt to the water and bless it: *'I purify thee, by the Moon that rules thee to aid me'.*

Present the photograph at the Four Gates, declaring the object of the rite. Then approach the altar and hold the photo the wrong way up, so that it is reflected in the water of the cauldron. Say:

> *By Astral light; by moon-beams bright,*
> *I charge the water, clear;*
> *To turn the tide for ---------(name)*
> *The face reflected here.*
>
> *The Moon will take away all strife;*
> *Commence another phase -*
> *A mirrored surface, smooth as glass,*
> *Will thus describe your days.*

With hope serene within your breast,
Forget all hurt and pain;
Emerge from oceans newly-born,
And laugh at life, again.

Look at the face in the water and 'see' the person in whatever happy or loving conditions you wish for them. Build the appropriate scenery or people round them and hold that picture for at least ten minutes. Then relax your will, and rest.

Invocations, Chants and Prayers

The Cycle of the Moon
by Arnold Crowther

High Priestess stands in front of the altar wearing black cloak of invisibility. Maiden (or Server) strikes bell and recites on knees. All witches kneel.

O! lovely Goddess of the Moon,
Enfolded in the arms of the Black Panther of the night;
We pray you grant this world a boon,
And make our darkness visible, with all your shining light.

Cast off your pitch-black mantle,
And turn night into day;
For we are lost without you, to guide us on our way.

A silver light breaks through the clouds,
We'll see the Goddess soon,
And slowly She'll appear to us, in the phases of the Moon.

Priestess slowly lowers cloak, just in line with her breasts; Maiden strikes bell, once:

The new Moon flickers in the sky;
The night conceals the rest,
Until the second-phase reveals
Her lovely well-formed breast.

Priestess lowers cloak to waist. Maiden strikes bell, twice:

Then comes the third phase of the Moon,
She drops Her cloak of night;
And stands there naked in the sky,
Her body shining bright.

Priestess lets cloak fall and stands in 'Goddess' position, with hands 'cupping' breasts. Maiden strikes bell, three times. All bow low:

If only you could stay with us,
And turn night into day;
The God calls from the Underworld,
The Goddess must obey.

Maiden lifts cloak and gives it to Priestess, who holds it to her waist. Maiden strikes bell, twice:

Take up the cloak of darkness,
Conceal once more your light;
The Moon is slowly on the wane,
Bad spirits haunt the night.

Priestess holds cloak to breasts. Maiden strikes bell, once:

The pale Moon slowly disappears,
The light will slowly die;
The Panther will devour his prey,
And darkness fill the sky.

ALL

As you go through the Underworld,
We honour you upon this Earth,
With prayers and chants and magic spells,
And wait once more for your re-birth.

Blessed Be!

(The above rite can also be worked by two people (male and female), or by one witch, employing it as an invocation.)

Invocation to the Goddess

Circle Chant by Patricia Crowther

We invoke Thee Queen of Queens,
Aradia! Aradia!

Come to us in all our dreams,
Aradia! Aradia!

Blessed Goddess from above,
Aradia! Aradia!

Grant us peace and grant us love.
Aradia! Aradia!

Heed Thy children here below,
Aradia! Aradia!

Let us all Thy secrets know,
Aradia! Aradia!

Perfect love and perfect trust,
Aradia! Aradia!

Less would turn all into dust.
Aradia! Aradia!

Let the Mill keep spinning round,
Aradia! Aradia!

The Wheel of Life where all are bound,
Aradia! Aradia!

Upwards, upwards, on and on,
Aradia! Aradia!

Till our souls with Thee are One!
Aradia! Aradia!

Nearer, nearer, nearer, come -
EH-OH-AH-EE-AH-OHH-UM!

(The Dance should cease before the sonics are intoned at the end. Or, alternatively, the chant can be repeated three or five times; only stopping at the final vowel sounds. The name Aradia is pronounced: ar-A-dia, with the accent on the middle A.)

The Witches' Sabbath

By Arnold Crowther

Come horse, come hound, come leaping toads,
Down from the forests and over the roads,
Through all the meadows and over the ditches;
Off to the Sabbath to dance with the witches.
Beavers and badgers and nocturnal creatures;
Cats, bats and howlets with comical features,
Flying and creeping and crawling and walking,

Dancing and singing and laughing and talking.
Folks come from the cottages, people with riches
Come altogether to dance with the witches.
Flowers from the hedges with mosses and lichen
Carried by ladies and maids from the kitchen;
Squires from the manors and boys from the stable,
Young folk and old folk and all who are able,
Travel by twilight avoiding all hitches;
Everyone rushing to dance with the witches.
Round the bonfire they go merrily tripping,
Yelling and screaming and jumping and skipping.
Free as the wind they keep dancing and shrieking,
Bodies all gleaming and sweating and reeking.
This is far better than all of your riches;
Throw off your cares and let's dance with the witches.
In the pale moonlight they romp till the morning,
When everybody is tired out and yawning.
Loudly they shout in the highest of pitches,
'O for the nights when we dance with the witches!'

Old Hornie

By Arnold Crowther

When the Autumn winds do blow,
Through the forest we all go;
Chasing deer or stag or doe,
Hunting with Old Hornie!

O'er the bracken, through the burn,
Up the brae and then a turn;
That's the sport for which we yearn,
Hunting with Old Hornie!

Nags all sweating as they leap
Fences, ditches, crags so steep;

While the villagers all sleep,
We hunt with Old Hornie!

'Twang!' the arrows leave each bow,
Swiftly through the air they go;
Bringing down a hart or doe,
Hunting with Old Hornie!

Knives go flashing through the hide,
As the carcass they divide;
And to a woodland glen they ride,
Hunting with Old Hornie!

Fires are lighted for the roast,
Horns are raised to drink a toast;
Hunters all propose their host -
Our hunting god - 'Old Hornie!'

Let us raise our goblets high,
'Neath a grey October sky,
And in boisterous voice all cry -
'Here's to you - Old Hornie!'

Song of the Seasons

Words by Arnold Crowther

We dig and we plough and we hoe and we sow,
It's best done in moonlight as you ought to know,
We pray to the Goddess to make the seeds grow;
Singing: 'too rali oo rali oo rali o'.

We fill up the furrows, the seeds lie below,
With patience we wait though they germinate slow,
Then all of a sudden the seeds start to grow;
Singing: 'too rali oo rali oo rali o'.

The Sun shines upon them, they're all doing fine,
The crops of the fields are all growing in line,
They shoot through the earth and they all start to show;
Singing: 'too rali oo rali oo rali o'.

We get on our broomsticks and dance round the field,
This causes the meadows to give and to yield,
The higher we jump and the higher they grow;
Singing: 'too rali oo rali oo rali o'.

And then comes the harvest when all things are ripe,
We honour the Goddess with song, drum and pipe,
And gather the crops in before we get snow;
Singing: 'too rali oo rali oo rali o'.

So praise be the Goddess who makes all things thrive,
And gives us the fodder by which we survive,
We give adoration before She must go;
Singing: 'too rali oo rali oo rali o'.

With Winter upon us, Old Hornie comes back,
When evenings are long and the nights are pitch black,
And all of the country is covered in snow;
Singing: 'too rali oo rali oo rali o'.

So give him so homage and also a cheer,
And hope he will not make the Winter severe,
With Springtime, the Goddess will come back we know;
Singing: 'too rali oo rali oo rali o'.

Prayer to the Goddess

By Patricia Crowther

O Mother of all living,
Pour out Thy store of wondrous things.
Help Thy children to know Thee in all Thy ways;
Give then sight and wisdom on their path through life.
Let them not falter in their faith and constancy,
But know, that Thou art a part of them,
As they are of Thee.
Grant us Thy blessing, O! sweet Goddess,
That by our worship Thou wil't be forever, revered.

My Law - Tieme Ranapiri

The sun may be clouded, yet ever the sun
Will sweep on its course till the Cycle is run.
And when into chaos the system is hurled
Again shall the Builder reshape a new world.

Your path may be clouded, uncertain your goal:
Move on - for your orbit is fixed to your soul.
And though it may lead into darkness of night
The torch of the Builder shall give it new light.

You were. You will be! know this while you are:
Your spirit has travelled both long and afar.
It came from the Source, to the Source it returns -
The Spark which was lighted eternally burns.

It slept in a jewel. It leapt in a wave.
It roamed in the forest. It rose from the grave.
It took on strange garbs for long eons of years
And now in the soul of yourself It appears.

From body to body your spirit speeds on
It seeks a new form when the old one has gone
And the form that it finds is the fabric you wrought,
On the look of the Mind from the fibre of Thought.

As dew is drawn upwards, in rain to descend
Your thoughts drift away and in Destiny blend.
You cannot escape them, for petty or great,
Or evil or noble, they fashion your Fate.

Somewhere on some planet, sometime and somehow
Your life will reflect your thoughts of your Now.
My Law is unerring, no blood can atone -
The structure you built you will live in - alone.

From cycle to cycle, through time and through space
Your lives with your longings will ever keep pace.
And all that you ask for, and all you desire
Must come at your bidding, as flame out of fire.

Once list' to that Voice and all tumult is done -
Your life is the Life of the Infinite One.
In the hurrying race you are conscious of pause
With love for the purpose, and love for the Cause.

You are your own Devil, you are your own God
You fashioned the paths your footsteps have trod.
And no one can save you from Error or Sin
Until you have hark'd to the Spirit within.

Attributed to a Maori

1. Patricia Crowther. (photo Gwion)

2a. The White Horse at Uffington, Berkshire (By permission of Aerofilms Ltd)

2b. Horse and Rider. Cast in Sheffield stainless steel by Scrata, this statue was created by David Wynne and inspired by the White Horse of Uffington. (Photo J Edward Vickers O.B.E.)

3. The Stone Goddess, discovered in 1976 at Castleton, Derbyshire. (By courtesy of Peter Harrison. Photo J Edward Vickers O.B.E.)

4. A vase depicting the 'Green Man' the witches' God of the woodlands. (Author's collection, photo by J Edward Vickers O.B.E.)

5a. The 'Green Man' of Fountains Abbey, Yorkshire. Thought to be the only known picture. (Photo John H Cutton)

5b. The Cerne Giant, Cerne Abbas, Dorset. (By permission of Aerofilms Ltd)

6a. *The cottage in St Albans, Herts, used by Gerald Gardner as a covenstead. (Author's collection)*

6b. 'Off to the Sabbat' a painting by Gerald Gardner. (Author's collection, *Photo J Edward Vickers O.B.E.*)

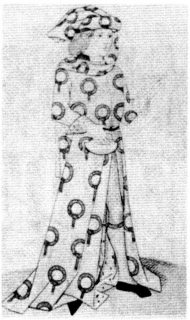

7. *A Knight of the Garter, a fifteenth century drawing.* (Author's collection)

8. 'The Goddess of the Moon', a painting by Arnold Crowther

9. The author in ritual dress and pose. (Photo Gwion)

7 The Sacred Site

It may be your intention to work out-of-doors on occasions when the weather permits! If so, it would be very silly to go 'sky-clad', especially in the British climate. Most witches wear a warm, hooded robe over their clothes for these meetings, which is the most sensible way of approaching the matter.

The robe is usually tied round the waist with a cord or girdle, which prevents the cold air from penetrating, and also keeps the garment in place. A cloak would not serve the same purpose, being apt to swirl out during any movements, and could be dangerous if there is a fire of any description.

Speaking of fire, an excellent device to make possible the use of candles out-of-doors is the camper's lantern. This has four glass panels to protect the flame, and can be employed to mark the four quarters.

A rite of this kind usually involves some considerable trouble to arrange; but, believe me, it is well worth it. A summer's night under a full moon, all nature round you, and the earth beneath your feet, takes some beating, for a Sabbat or Esbat.

The first thing is to find your own particular site. An Ordnance Survey map will give you the location of sacred sites and stone circles in your area. A visit to the chosen site in daylight is essential to see if it is a suitable place, to find the best way to reach it at night, to discover how long it would take to arrive safely in the dark, and to observe the ground surface. If there are bumps and odd stones around, this could result in a ricked ankle or some other accident. So be sure of these things before you decide on a site. Then, too, there is the 'feel' of the place; the vibes which will tell you whether or not it has been visited by less well-intentioned folk.

There may be a local wood which has a glade or clear space in the centre; it does not have to be a circle. You can be 'at one' with the powers of nature anywhere in the countryside.

Hills and high places were regarded as holy, partly because of the climb, which was enacted physically as well as mentally! Certainly, there are many hill-figures which substantiate this idea. And many of them have a round indentation of ground above them, which, in some places, country folk consider to be haunted, or, in some way, uncanny. This is probably because they were used in olden times, and still preserve the power.

Dowsers have touched certain stones and received a kind of electric shock from them. And we know that stones carry memory and store energy, as testified by the work of T.C. Lethbridge and others.

Look for places with old names; places with names which link with the Old Gods. Folk-memory dies hard in the country, and often a name will lead you in the right direction.

Most of the hill-figures are said to be made over Ley Lines, or where certain earth energies merge. These include, the White Horse at Uffington, Berkshire; the Cerne Giant, at Cerne Abbas in Dorset, and the Long Man, of Wilmington, in Sussex.

It is obvious that we have lost a lot of these figures over the years. Lethbridge tells us how he helped to excavate some hill-figures at Wandlebury near Cambridge. They found at least three; one, of the Mother Goddess - Ma Gog - seemingly seated on a white horse. The lady has more than two breasts, echoing Diana of Ephesus, the many-breasted one. The hills around Wandlebury are smooth and rounded, like those known as the Paps of Anu in Ireland, and the Cailleach Paps on Jura.

There is a similar situation on the top of the Wilmington Long Man. It is a tough climb to the top, but it is ideal as a working site. A hollow of flat ground, with two small hillocks at the back, suggests that it was man-made in the image of the Earth Mother.

My husband and I, along with some witch friends, have had quite a few enjoyable Esbats up there. On the last occasion some years ago, the ceremony resulted in the following poem, which I wrote immediately upon waking the next day. Hence its title:

Awakening

Perhaps you and I in ages long,
Walked together with hidden song,
And worshipped the One, the One of Three,
By Oak and Ash and Rowan tree.

Perhaps we danced till dawn did break,
And all the birds in gladness wake;
Perhaps we knew the secrets wise,
To stir the blood and reach the skies.

Could it be true that we are met
Again, in Nemesis gilded net;
To foil once more the darkened pit,
And give us sense to conquer it?

When one has communed with the forces of life, especially at a sacred site, it often has the effect of evoking some form of creative art. A friend of mine painted a most beautiful psychic picture after one such meeting.

The Rollright circle was a regular meeting-place for witches until a group of teenagers set fire to one of the stones. Admission was then confined to certain daylight hours.

Speaking of the Rollrights, I have found from experience, that the group of stones known as the Whispering Knights often give answers to your questions. These are received psychically, of course, yet 'speak' they do, and in very down-to-earth terms, while their atmosphere is quite unique. It has been suggested that originally they had a capstone, and the structure was used by the local seer, which would account for their receptiveness. Of course, the approach to these stones must be one of complete faith and reverence, any offering being given in trust and love.

It was during a drive in the same district that a friend took me to see a long barrow. The burial chamber had long fallen in and it was surrounded with bushes and bright yellow gorse. We walked round it and I suddenly saw a figure which had been drawn in the light, sandy soil. It was of human proportions, with what looked like a wide-brimmed hat on its head. The face was etched in a smile, and we were surprised to see that it was an hermaphrodite, with a phallus and female breasts. Nearby, we found some twisted ears of corn, which had been bent towards the figure and were wedged between stones to keep them firm.

We deduced it to be some kind of fertility magic, the figure had both male and female attributes. This connects with some statues of the Old Gods, who were depicted in the same way to represent the duality of the Godhead. There was also the hat, which was similar to the one worn by the Magician, in the Tarot. Among other things, this card equates with Aries, the beginning of the Tide of Activation (see Tides). Our assumption may, or may not, have been the correct one, but this discovery shows the continuance of magic in the heart of rural England!

On the top of Trendle Hill in Dorset stands the huge figure of the Cerne Giant. About 180 feet high and 45 feet across, he stands with erect club and penis, defiantly, unashamed. And yet the figure provides an aura of peace and well-being, the outstretched left hand being open and welcoming.

It is a local saying that couples who find it difficult to have babies should go up the hill at night and make love on his phallus, and I have heard several instances of this act being effective!

There is a story told in those parts about two nuns who asked a local farmer the way up to the Giant. His reply to their question was, 'It be no use trying for bairns 'til't Spring!'

A one-time clergyman of Cerne Abbas was affronted at the Giant's sexual frankness and tried to have that part of his anatomy ploughed up. But he received such opposition from the people of the surrounding districts that he gave up the attempt. 'If you do that, our crops will fail', they told him.

There was always a folk-festival each Spring on the top of the Giant, with the traditional maypole dances, until the local clergy succeeded in banning it. They were of the opinion that too much licentious behaviour went into the celebration!

The scouring of these hill-figures took place every seven years. Seven is the number of spiritual things. At the White Horse near Uffington, an old Berkshire ballad was sung while the work was in progress:

> *The owl White Horse wants zetting to rights,*
> *And the Square hav promised good cheer;*
> *Zo we'll gee un a scrape to kip un in shape,*
> *And a'll last for many a year.*

It was quite an occasion, as after the cleaning the lord of the manor would give a feast and entertain the workers; in fact it was his duty to do so. There was also a fair and all kinds of sporting activities which lasted for almost a week.

White horses were always sacred to the Mother Goddess, also known as the Mare Goddess. People describe bad dreams as *night-mares*; these occur when the dark, hidden aspects of the mind, which are stored in the subconscious, are released, sometimes during sleep. The subconscious mind links with the Crone, or Hag of the Dark Moon and holds our deepest, sometimes sinister, thoughts.

Turning to more pleasant things, horseshoes have been considered lucky since ancient times, particularly because of their shape, symbolical of the crescent moon and the seven nails with which they are secured.

Iron Age coins depict a horse with a crescent moon above it, and in the Pin Hole Cave in Derbyshire, a piece of bone was found which shows a man wearing a horse- mask.

The Godiva rider, a young, virgin girl, would ride upon a white horse at the Spring festival. White, being a symbol of purity, could be one reason for the sacredness of this animal. But the curious fact is that the British people have always refused to eat horsemeat, even when food was scarce.

The superb contour of the Uffington horse is made with only five lines in a stencil-like accuracy. The effect is one of beauty as it leaps across the downs. Pure poetry!

The White Horse is some 3,000 years old, and the strange thing about it - and, indeed, some of the other hill-figures - is that it can only be seen, in proper perspective from the air! The whole area is steeped in strange places and legends. It is said that to stand on the eye of the Horse (a large flat stone) and turn round three times while making a wish, brings good luck. Now it is fairly evident that local superstitions are the remnants of some ancient knowledge. Guy Underwood says all these figures were raised on places where the geodetic lines of earth energy, or Ley Lines, converged. And he also says that the eye of the Horse is placed exactly above a blind spring!

Behind the design is a great hill fort, and not far away in the valley is a large artificial mound called Dragon's Hill. The atmosphere of the area is ideally expressed in G.K. Chesterton's 'Ballad of the White Horse' which begins:

> *Before the gods that made the gods*
> *Had seen their sunrise pass,*
> *The White Horse of the White Horse Vale,*
> *Was cut out of the grass.*

> *Before the gods that made the gods,*
> *Had drunk at dawn their fill,*
> *The White Horse of the White Horse Vale,*
> *Was hoary on the hill.*

> *Age beyond age on British land,*
> *Aeons on aeons gone,*
> *Was peace and war in Western hills,*
> *And the White Horse looked on ....*

It is quite possible that the witches of olden times knew about this earth energy and its effects, because many ancient sites are associated with them: places such as the famous Pendle Hill, the stamping ground of the Lancashire witches, and Chanctonbury Ring in Sussex, a well-known meeting-place for witches past and present. Bredon Hill near Tewkesbury is another. These hills were sacred and were most probably the esoteric centres of the Old Religion.

Michael Dames has made an invaluable contribution to this subject which is set out in his two books *The Avebury Cycle* and *The Silbury Treasure*. Here is someone who has looked at these two monuments with eyes other than those of previous archaeologists and examiners. Silbury Hill is the largest man-made mound in Western Europe and it has been excavated at various periods of history in the hope of finding a royal tomb!

In 1723, the antiquarian William Stukeley employed a local workman to keep his eyes open for anything of interest when some trees were being planted on the hill. They came across a burial just below the surface, but Stukeley dismissed it as being the legendary body of King Sil, whose tomb Silbury was supposed to be. Subsequent digs were made by the Duke of Northumberland in 1776; John Merewether, Dean of Hereford in 1849; Sir W.M. Flinders-Petrie in 1922; Dr. F.R. McKim in 1959, and, last but not least, Professor R.J.C. Atkinson and BBC 2 in 1967.

As Michael Dames comments, all the interest in Silbury was confined to a patriarchal hero/treasure syndrome. No one ever conceived the possibility of the hill being anything but the grave of a warrior king with attendant hoard of gold and treasure. But Dames shows Silbury Hill to be an exact representation of the Great Goddess, the whole area having been erected and arranged to depict this phenomena. The hill itself is her pregnancy, while the surrounding moat describes her body! His book on Silbury includes photographs which substantiate this discovery in no uncertain terms. And the complete figure is expressed in exactly the same manner as the stone statues of the goddess in Neolithic art-forms, namely, as a squatting female about to give birth. The Silbury goddess is about 4,000 years old and could be even older.

Dames suggests that the people gathered to watch the goddess giving birth. This was at Lammas-time, when the earth is said to be in labour, with the Moon as the indicator of the sacred process, its movement covering the entire enactment with geometrical precision.

The hill was made as a great web, building up to a flat summit and an indentation on the top, which Dames links with the womb/eye symbolism of Neolithic peoples, reflecting the eye of intelligence and the eye of birth.

The 'child' is born when the Moon indicates the inter-causeway ditch, the lunar disc appearing as the 'head' in the water. There is also an astronomical, geometric link with Avebury, which is intriguing in its implications.

The Lammas moon is the first full moon after the solar quarter-day, and is probably the time when the building of the hill was initiated. This theory is substantiated by the fact that winged ants, which fly in August, were found at its core.

You will notice the repeated occurrence of the name Nine Maidens, or Nine Ladies, given to stone circles throughout the land. Again, the number of stones links with the number of the Moon, and the three aspects of the Goddess, each aspect presided over by three females. A theory which has been put forward, suggests that three women tended the sacred fire in the Circle; three looked for fuel, while the remaining three, rested. The fire was never allowed to go out, as it provided warmth, kept wild animals at bay, and was a means of cooking food. Gods and men lived very closely together in ancient times, and there was no thought of keeping religion and everyday life separate. Which is why witchcraft symbols often incorporate a practical, as well as a religious use: artifacts such as the pitch-fork, horseshoe, cauldron and broomstick.

Places such as crossroads, or where three ways met, have always been connected with witches and their rites. The goddess as Dea-Triformis of the Cross Ways, Hecate Triformis, or the Three Ladies of Britain, was often presented with gifts or offerings which were left at such places. The Athenians had a public supper every month, which was laid out where three ways met.

If you find such a spot in the countryside be very careful that a passing motorist does not drive roughshod over you. Today's traffic is very different from the horse and cart and carriages of yesteryear.

Speaking of crossroads leads me to the famous Irish witch, Lady Alice Le Kyteler, because the records of her trial in 1324 show her to have performed certain rituals at these places.

She is said to have sacrificed nine red cocks and nine peacock's eyes to a spirit named Robin Filius Artis (Robin, Son of Art), which she scattered at a crossroads. Lady Alice and her coven also had a 'wooden beam called a coulter', which after she had rubbed it with a magic ointment, could be used for flying to any place they chose!

She is also reported to have engaged in acts of sympathetic magic. One such was the sweeping of the streets of Kilkenny between compline and twilight, raking all the dirt and refuse to her son's door, muttering secretly to herself:

To the house of William my sone,
Hie all the wealth of Kilkennie towne.

Compline was the last religious service of the day, but notice the number *nine* again in the above ritual. The peacock's eyes were most probably the tail-feathers of these birds, long associated with magic and considered by some to be unlucky. They certainly look like eyes and have a strange beauty which has bestowed upon them uncanny influences. Now, Robin Artisson is said to have been Dame Alice's lover, so he could hardly have been a spirit, in the real sense of the word. The whole coven numbered thirteen people, which again shows the authenticity and age of witchcraft ceremonies.

This was Ireland's first important witch-trial, and I mention it here because of a curious piece of information I came across some years ago.

Lady Alice was a woman of high social status, with many influential supporters, and she succeeded, through their help, to escape to England, where nothing more was heard of her. But in a book of Yorkshire legends, published by Dalesman, I read, that at Clapdale Hall (once Clapdale Castle) there lived one John de Clapham, and, nearby, at the foot of Trow Gill, there was a tiny cottage where lived a Dame Alice Ketyll, his foster mother. Owing to the poor fortunes of John de Clapham, she is said to have invoked the Devil, who called upon a Robin Artisson to be her familiar spirit. She then promised to sweep the old Clapham bridge between compline and curfew and proceeded to rake all the dust towards the castle with the words:

> *Into the house of John, my sone,*
> *Hie all the wealth of Clapham Towne.*

Further, the legend tells how she took nine red cocks, freshly killed, and put them in a ring around her on the bridge!

After reading this account, I wrote to the publishers of the book, and was told that it was a collection of legends and stories of the county gathered from many sources. So I put an advertisement in the *Dalesman* magazine asking for information re Clapham in Craven. I duly received a letter from a descendant of the Clapham family, who told me of a Thomas Clapham who married Elizabeth More of Otterburn. Her mother, Thomasine, was the daughter of Sir Peter Mauleverer, and Elizabeth inherited the family fortune. There were four sons of the marriage, the eldest of whom was John de Clapham. The date of his birth was around 1327, so if indeed the Dame Alice Ketyll of Clapdale and the Lady Alice Le Kyteler who fled to England are one and the same, we have solved the mystery of her disappearance!

Clapham in Craven is only twenty miles from the West coast and the Irish Sea and is buried deep in wooded country. If the Clapham legend is true, Dame Alice may have arrived there at the time of John's birth, and in due course became his foster mother. Notice that she did not live at the Hall, but in a tiny cottage in the woods where she could be away from inquisitive eyes.

In *Brigantia*, by Guy Ragland Phillips, mention is made of Bolton Priory where the Clapham family were interred upright! Phillips also writes about the time that the BBC were making a film in the area. Two of the team stayed in Clapdale Hall, which was then derelict, and had heard a tradition of some knights of the Claphams. The story was that they had been buried upright, in full armour, beneath the Hall itself.

Using a metal detector, they found that it definitely reacted at one section of the floor. The operator, a Mr. Wooding, was suddenly seized with a feeling of terror as of an evil presence and fled out of the house to drop exhausted several yards away.

Phillips says local people are afraid of the Hall, which all seems to point to some kind of magical activities connected with the Clapham family in the past. Perhaps Lady Alice was helped and protected by her own kind! (For a full account of the Kyteler trial, see *An ABC of Witchcraft* by Doreen Valiente.)

In his book, Phillips describes the area of Brigantia, in ancient times, as spreading from the Wash to Dumfries. The whole of 'Brigantia' is covered with innumerable sacred sites which, quite literally, pepper the vast tract of land. The book also gives the alignments of Ley Lines, one of which finishes at Whitby Abbey.

The Green Man is much in evidence in the North of England: one of the most beautiful representations is the stone head at Fountains Abbey which has boughs issuing from the mouth, while at Hutton-in-the-Forest near Penrith, there is a similar carving above an ancient well. Goddess figures abound too, and some little known ones have been unearthed by Phillips.

Other expressions of early man in the North of England include the Swastica Stone, Ilkley Moor; the Tree of Life Stone, Snowden Carr; Brimham Rocks, Nidderdale; Jenny Twigg and her Daughter Tib; and the immense phallic menhirs at Boroughbridge and Rudston.

Brimham Rocks are fantastic shapes; their great bulks balancing on quite tiny, waisted pedestals, with strange markings on their bases. They rest of Ley Lines and the mystique of the place marks it as being an ancient site. The local people have regarded them with awe for a very long time; the rocks are thought to house a spirit which is friendly, and known as the Son of the Rocks.

On Fountains Moor, two great uprights, which look like giantesses in broad bonnets, reign supreme. These rocks are called Jenny Twigg and her Daughter Tib - very aptly, I think. The name 'Jenny' has many associations with pagan places in Yorkshire and was, quite probably, an old synonym for the Goddess in those parts.

Gerald Gardner had the ideal solution to the problem of finding a suitable site. He bought an old cottage in

Buckinghamshire, and had it transported to some private woods near St. Albans, of which he was part owner. Gerald used it solely for a covenstead, and the atmosphere, amid the surrounding trees, couldn't have been better. I once attended a meeting there, and often wonder if it is still utilized by the local coven.

I wish you luck in finding your own special place; but do remember to leave it unspoilt; and if you must light a fire, use the cauldron for safety.

8 The Tides

The Sun and the Moon have a great effect upon the Earth, and so do the planets, each reflecting a virtue and influence peculiar to themselves. To obtain the maximum effect from the Planetary Rites in this book, it is advantageous to perform them at the best time, i.e. when the Powers of Life are 'on your side', so to speak. There are times too for raising power and times for absorbing power.

There are many aspects which can be observed, but here are the major ones.

(a) An understanding of the Seasonal Tides.

(b) The Planet of a particular rite should be well aspected.

(c) The Lunar Tide should be auspicious.

(d) The Planetary Periods should be observed.

The Tides, effective on the physical Plane, are also effective on the Astral Plane and in the Astral Light. Thus it will be seen how important it is to work with them.

There is no need to inform members of the Craft of the advantages of working with the powers of Nature, as besides understanding these phenomena today, it can be proved that the followers of the Old Religion in ancient times knew of them also. How? By simply observing the times of the four Greater Sabbats: Beltane, Lughnassadh, Samhain and Oimelc or Imbolc.

As will be seen from the diagram, of 'The Witches Wheel' on page 110, they occur exactly between the solstices and equinoxes, or should do! The solstices and equinoxes are fixed by natural phenomena i.e. by the longest and shortest days, and by the day and nights of equal length, respectively. These times are known as the Lesser Sabbats, being adopted as festivals much later than the Greater Sabbats, and were, in the main, times for merrymaking rather than magic making.

The solstices naturally celebrated the Sun and its increase and decrease. The Vernal Equinox represented the new beginning: Eostra returns. The Autumn Equinox heralded the approach of Winter; the last fling before the Great Huntsman arrives!

So much for the natural phenomena. But with the change-over from the old calendar to the new Gregorian calendar, twelve days were lost. So the present dates for the Greater Sabbats, 30 April, 1 August, 31 October and 2 February are twelve days behind the old Calendar.

They also fall short of the peak of the seasonal tides, which is at 15 degrees of the fixed signs of the Zodiac. The rhythm of the tides can easily be calculated by observing that the Sun 'travels' 90 degrees from the Spring Equinox to the Summer Solstice. Halfway, at 45 degrees, we find Beltane at 15 degrees of Taurus, the date being 12 May. Lughnassadh at 15 degrees of Leo, is around 14 August; Samhain at 15 degrees of Scorpio, 12 November, and Oimelc at 15 degrees of Aquarius, approximately 14 February.

These dates are still a few days behind the old ones, but obviously, over an immense period of time, this slight discrepancy can be accounted for. Certainly, the old dates would seem to be the more accurate ones, and many covens still adhere to the old dates as being the truer times for holding the Greater Sabbats.

This seasonal power is transformed and modified by the four fixed signs of the Zodiac; or to put it a better way, the signs show in what manner the power is being *activated*.

In Taurus the Bull, the energy is fixed in the Earth itself. It is literally pushing life into being - into formation. So, Beltane is the Festival of Life; hence in ancient times, the celebration of the Sacred Marriage. A good time to work with new ideas and to be-coming a true individual.

The sign of Leo the Lion rules the flowering, fruitful time: Lughnassadh (or Lammas) when the Earth is in labour, delivering her bounty with generosity and love. Leo rules the Heart, so a chance to give help and love and communicate with others.

In the two remaining festivals, Samhain and Oimelc, the power is negative and positive respectively; but the accent is upon a spiritual level. Samhain, (Hallowe'en) in Scorpio, the sign of Death and Regeneration. The time to look beyond the Veil of Life, seeking rapport with Godhead and links with loved ones in Summerland.

In Aquarius and the Airy emanations of the Spirit shines the delicate light of the solitary flame symbolizing the Soul. This darkest period of reflection and rest is Oimelc (Candlemas), the purification festival of the Virgin Goddess, Brigid, a time to receive a renewal of spiritual strength.

It can be seen from the above that there are many ways in which the powers of the Greater Sabbats can be utilized. The Seasonal Tides are, in point of fact, magnetic currents which circulate the Earth from the North Pole to the South Pole. They merge and become neutral at the solstices and equinoxes, i.e. at each 90 degrees. From the Winter Solstice to the Summer Solstice the Tides are positive; the remaining two being negative.

THE WITCHES WHEEL.

HORNED GODDESS
Sun at Zenith

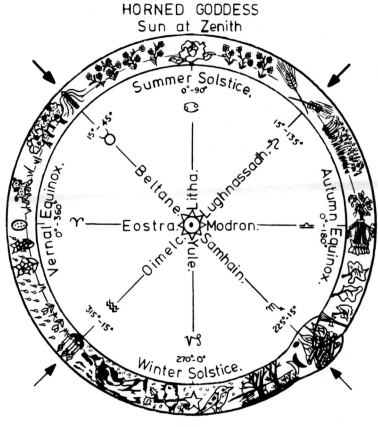

HORNED GOD
Sun at Nadir

By Leon Dickens

Although the Tide from the Winter Solstice to the Vernal Equinox is a positive one, it is yet one of the most dangerous for any active magical work. It is the most spiritual and fit only for the uses mentioned above.

It will be noticed, even in Christian art-forms, how the four symbolic emblems of the fixed signs continually occur. Ezekiel, the Biblical prophet, had a vision of a flaming wheel with four faces upon it. They were those of a man (Aquarius), a bull (Taurus), a lion (Leo) and an eagle (the higher aspect of Scorpio). The secret is that the signs of Aquarius, Taurus, Leo and Scorpio contain the Four Gates of Avataric Descent. They are the Gates for a release of cosmic power and quite possibly could be the means of descent into matter, for an Avatar or Teacher! The very fact that the four oldest religious festivals of Western Europe take place in the middle of these Zodiac signs is surely proof enough of our ancestors' knowledge and wisdom.

On 5 February 1962 a rare occurrence took place in the sign of Aquarius. The seven major planets, Saturn, Jupiter, Mars, the 'Sun', 'Venus', 'Mercury' and the 'Moon', were all gathered in this sign. Astrologers considered this to be an event of great significance. Some of them said it could indicate the birth of a new spiritual leader who would represent the ideals of the Aquarian Age, especially as the great conjunction was in Aquarius itself.

It has even more significance when one realizes the implications of it occurring in one of the most spiritual tides, that of Avataric Descent.

If, indeed, such a birth took place, it is interesting to note that the new ruling planet of Aquarius, namely Uranus, was in Leo, the sign of leadership, on that date; while Neptune, the mystical planet, was occupying Scorpio, the sign of regeneration!

Taking the premise a little further, conception of the birth would have occurred in Taurus, yet another Avataric Gate! Both of these tides are positive ones and there is also the strange connection with the Old Religion. In ancient times, children conceived in the May-time festivities were born in February, at the festival of Candlemas or Oimelc, presided over by the Goddess in her role of Protectoress of Childbirth!

Other astrologers viewed the conjunction as an indication of the beginning of the New Age, although this is disputed by some people. It was also pointed out that as Aquarius is the 'human' sign of the Zodiac, the omen showed us the way we must take, if our planet and its people are to survive. In other words, we must cease our present discord and strife, and become tolerant to all nations. In fact, we must redeem *ourselves!*

This 'message ' is also in accordance with the prophecy of the Age of Aquarius; that 'every man will become his own saviour'!

The next important point to observe when performing the Planetary Rites is to note if a planet is well-aspected at the time. This can be checked upon very easily, but the following list may be of help.

Saturn	Ruler of Capricorn; exalted in Libra; detriment Cancer; fall Aries.
Jupiter	Ruler of Sagittarius; benevolent in Pisces; exalted in Cancer; detriment Gemini; fall Capricorn.
Mars	Ruler of Aries, and by tradition Scorpio (more recently attributed to Pluto); exalted in Capricorn; detriment Libra; fall Cancer.

The Sun	Ruler of Leo; exalted in Aries; detriment Aquarius; fall Libra.
Venus	Ruler of Taurus and Libra; exalted in Pisces; detriment Aries; fall Virgo.
Mercury	Ruler of Gemini and Virgo; exalted in Virgo; detriment Sagittarius; fall Pisces.
The Moon	Ruler of Cancer; exalted in Taurus; detriment Capricorn; fall Scorpio.

The Lunar Tides are auspicious in all but the 'Dark of the Moon', this is the phase from the end of the Waning, to the appearance of the next New Moon. The best period in which to work is when the Moon is full, the phases of the New Moon and the first quarter being also beneficial for initiating new magical ventures.

According to astrology, from 1945 to 1981 we were in the Aquarian Cycle of the Piscean Age. The ruler of that cycle was the Moon; thus the Moon was said to be working through the sign of Aquarius.

The Moon symbolizes *change* in all its forms. There were many happenings of lunar influence during that particular cycle. 'Equality for women', was the cry, and not before time! The birth of the Women's Liberation Movement, the renaissance of the Old Religion, with its worship of the feminine forces of life, personified by the Moon Goddess, were only a few of them.

One of the most wonderful achievements has been man's landing on the Moon itself. This age-old dream has been fulfilled, and a strange thing happened on the day man set foot upon the orb: Professor Iris Love found a temple of the moon goddess, near the Aegean sea!

In Britain, we had the Prime Minister Edward Heath, a Cancerian, born under the Moon. He took us into the Common Market, which made *nine* countries in all.

To mark the occasion a new fifty-pence coin was minted. Britannia has been given the sack on this one, being replaced by a circle of nine joined hands. If you look closely, you will see that there are eight masculine hands, but the ninth one is a feminine hand, symbolizing the Mother Country!

In occultism, nine has always been the number of the Moon, and recently it has been recorded that the Moon measures 2,160 miles across. Add these digits up; they come to *nine*.

The Moon rules the masses of the people, the home and the family. It takes nine moons for a baby to be born. The desires of the man-in-the street have overruled and swayed the decisions of the Establishments in many countries all over the globe.

Aquarius stands for the powers of the mind: tolerance, freedom and reformation. On the negative side, this fixed air sign can be unpredictable, eccentric and perverse.

Uranus (the ruler of Aquarius) and the Moon made a formidable partnership, the chief traits being a hatred for any kind of control and an extreme dislike of conventionality. All this proclaimed by the great conjunction in the middle of that Cycle.

The final aspects which may be observed are the Planetary Periods. These concern the dividing of each day and night of the week into twenty-four divisions. Each division is ruled by one of the Planets in strict order of sequence.

The Planet after which the day is named always takes precedence over the others. For example, the first period of

Saturday is ruled by Saturn; the first period of Friday, by Venus, and so on.

The times of the periods are calculated from sunrise to sunset (the day) and from sunset to sunrise (the night) and are roughly of one hour's duration. These times can be easily found by the perusal of a reputable ephemeris for the year in question. If Summer Time is in operation, remember to take one hour *off* the existing clock time.

A rite commenced in the correct planetary period may be found to overlap into the following one. But this does not detract from it, as it is the *commencement* of the rite which gives it its impetus. A table of the periods is included for those who would use the planetary forces to the full (see Appendix).

Tide of Activation (Positive)
Beltane

Beltane in the Tide of Activation is an excellent time to perform works connected with self-improvement at all levels. Ideas and plans concerning development and new beginnings, or refinement of the spiritual self, which manifests through the physical self.

The power is towards the Earth and earthly things. There is nothing against endeavouring to improve one's material status, or indeed of furthering ambitions by magical means. 'An it harm none, do what ye will!' The word for this period is *self-hood*.

Tide of Consolidation   (Negative)
Lughnassadh

The Tide of Consolidation is a time for giving and receiving. The joyousness of generosity in all its aspects is exemplified in the Cornucopia of the Earth's bounty, given freely and without any conditions. Gratitude and love from her children, is all that is asked at Lughnassadh. In the 'heart' of Leo we work for others, and they for us. The word is *benevolence*.

Tide of Recession   (Negative)
Samhain

The Tide of Recession informs us of Death. The power is receding into the unmanifest. The Festival of the Dead is celebrated with the Gate of Horn wide open to receive our loved ones from Summerland.

At this time we give power to the Gods to achieve a spiritual result. This is shown by the tail of the Scorpion and the sign. The word is *God-hood*.

Tide of Lustration   (Positive)
Oimelc

The Tide of Lustration is the darkest one on the material plane. No acts of magic are advisable during this Tide, as the power, although positive, is entirely spiritual and therefore, hidden. The impenetrable blackness of the void, of Nuit (or Nought) is accentuated by the solitary flame of the Virgin Goddess, Brigid. This is the light of illumination; therefore a period to be devoted to meditation. The word is *purification*.

(Oimelc is in the middle of February, a month which takes its name from *Februa* the latin word for purification.)

9 The Dance

The Dance is one of the oldest natural ways of attaining at-one-ment with the Divine. It allows free expression of the whole individual being. It can be performed alone, or in the company of others, and either method is effective.

For the lone practitioner the movement is a light tripping step, revolving on one's own axis. The invocation is performed first. The force invoked eventually fuses with the dancer's energy and produces the desired result. It must be reiterated that some of the easiest methods are the best, but practice is essential.

Circumambulation is a procedure which links with the pattern of the universe and is, therefore, sound on both spiritual and physical levels. It is in sympathy with the atoms, the stars and the slow march of the seasons.

In one of its aspects, that of Magic, it is the age-old method of raising the power and showing it what to do. The action is one of a generator and is the first and last expression of the Magic Circle.

The Dance can be performed in many ways and for many different reasons. The Round Dance, or Mill, is usually executed with the intention of raising power from the body and creating *rapport* between the coven members.

The Spiral, or Meeting Dance, is led by the High Priestess, guiding the people in a spiral pattern. As they pass each other, at given calls, kisses are exchanged.

The Spiral Dance, however, can be executed at a much deeper level. It links with the ancient maze-dance, and as the participants weave in and out the intent is to penetrate the Veil of Life and gain insight into the Inner Planes. This dance holds the key to death and re-birth. The witches hold a scarlet cord which is wound inwards to death and the beyond; it then coils back towards re-birth and life.

In Cretan myth, the goddess, Ariadne, used the same process to lead Theseus out of the labyrinth. She gave him a 'magic' ball of thread, which he unwound on his journey through to the centre of the maze. He there killed the Minotaur and with the help of the thread found his way out again.

If we assume myths to be a mixture of legend and allegory, we find the same reason behind this wondrous story: the journey through life to death; but man must destroy or conquer the animal side of his nature (the Minotaur, half-man, half-bull) in order to obtain immortality. This is made possible through the rites and worship of the Goddess, who holds the thread of life.

A fascinating book by James Vogh, entitled *Arachne Rising*, shows the 'lost' thirteenth sign of the Zodiac, as being a female spider-goddess, the Mistress of the Zodiac. In all mystical groups of thirteen people, there are twelve and the leader. In witchcraft there are twelve witches plus the priest or priestess, depending upon the time of year as to whether the God or Goddess is ruling. In the Middle Ages the leader was known as the 'Man in Black', who could be either male or female. Thus, in the Zodiac there are twelve signs, plus the Goddess with Her thread of Life, Death and Re-birth!

The ancient game of 'Nine Men's Morris' or Merelles was enacted upon a maze-like structure and is dated in the Bronze Age. Although it was a game, with nine men dressed in white and nine in black it was most probably evolved from a magical dance and the colours white and black could be connected with the Moon's phases.

Merelles was widely played in the Stratford-upon-Avon district. Shakespeare mentions it in 'A Midsummer Night's Dream', Act 2:1 -

> The fold stands empty in the drowned field
> And the crows are fatted with the murrain flock;
> The Nine Men's Morris is filled up with mud,
> And the quaint mazes in the wanton green,
> For lack of tread are indistinguishable.

Today, the game has been produced like a chess-board with wooden pegs to represent the men.

To obtain trance, the Dance of the Lame God is performed. This is a very slow circling, with the witches crossing their arms and linking hands. Could the performance of 'Auld Lang Syne' be a memory of this ancient witch dance? Especially, as it is sung at the time of year when the God of Death and Regeneration is ruling.

The dance is enacted by dragging the left (lame foot) behind the right, and moving slowly, deosil or sunwise, round the circle. The trance-state induced by this form of dance is preceded by a coldness which creeps up the body from the 'lame' foot. This coldness eventually overcomes the recipient and produces a deep trance. The person should be attended during the trance-state by an experienced witch, but should not be disturbed unless there are signs of distress. This is a very rare occurrence, but if it manifests, a gentle rubbing of the hands and feet, together with the person's name spoken softly and continuously, will bring the witch out of the trance.

Usually, there will be an Inner Plane experience for the entranced, or verbal messages which should be recorded.

Much depends upon the *reason* behind this dance, as to any potential results. The movement should be accompanied by a slow-worded chant, invoking the Horned God, and, ideally, performed at Samhain (Hallowe'en). In this way, contact can be made with the beloved dead and communication established.

Evidence from the witch-trials speak of an 'infamous' back-to-back dance. This seems to have been an abandoned frolic, with couples standing back-to-back, with linked arms. In this position they would prance around, occasionally stopping, when one partner would bend their back, lifting the other into the air. All this was accompanied by much screeching and shouting.

The author of *A Pleasant Treatise of Witches* says: '*The dance is strange, and wonderful, as well as diabolical, for turning themselves back to back, they take one another by the arms and raise each other from the ground, then shake their heads to and fro like Anticks, and turn themselves as if they were mad.*'

Why the author considers this type of dance to be diabolical is not known, but it is interesting to remember that precisely this form of movement was used in early Rock and Roll!

Marguerite Marquerie, a witness in a French trial in 1669, substantiates the above author as follows: '*Back to back and two by two, each witch has a wife of the Sabbat, which sometimes is his own wife, and these wives having been given to them when they were marked, they do not change them, this kind of dance being finished they dance hand in hand like our villagers.....*'

There was always music at these meetings which was usually provided by the use of a fiddle, pipe or cittern. In Somerset it is recorded that the witches danced to the tunes played on a pipe or cittern by the Man in Black. It is obvious from the above evidence that the witches were continuing an age-old pattern of worship and celebration.

Society in general had a very genteel way of dancing in the Middle Ages, the partners holding each other at arms length, only their hands being permitted to touch. Although there is no magical intent in the ordinary kinds of dancing, in any age, it seems very likely that the witches had some influence on modern forms.

Reginald Scott cites Bodin as remarking: *'these night-walking or rather night-dancing witches brought out of Italy into France, that dance which is called La Volta.'* La Volta is thought to have been the original form of the waltz, which was enhanced in time with the beautiful music of the Strauss family.

The Dance of Fertility is another very ancient idea. It predates most others and is an expression of sympathetic magic, the concept that like attracts like. Contrary to popular opinion, it was not usually performed for the propagation of the species, but for the fertility of the Earth. It necessitated the use of a Dancing Pole, which was placed between the legs and used like a hobby-horse. Very often it was carved in the shape of a phallus and greased with a special ointment.

There was much leaping into the air in order to encourage the crops to grow as tall. This may seem idiotic to modern minds, but it is now understood that all plant life grows much better with human love, care and attention. Science is continually substantiating and confirming things which the witches have known through millennia.

The Pole Dance was a definite prayer, but it was also combined with suitable action: the ancient idea that human energy must combine with the Divine to gain positive results.

There must be a link established between Inner and Outer Planes, between the spiritual and the physical.

The fertility dances have been replaced by folk customs and festivals. These customs differ, according to locality, yet all embrace some forgotten aspect of worship. There are literally thousands in Britain alone, which are enacted at various periods of the natural year, and which spring from the racial Unconscious.

The Dance of Fertility is best done out of doors, so that the witches have direct contact with the earth beneath their feet. The time for its performance is naturally at the beginning of the Tide of Activation (see Tides).

Most covens have their own particular chants and prayers for this dance, but for others who are interested in pursuing or investigating its validity, the following old chant is included:

As high as we jump,
So high will they grow,
Around and around
And around, we go.

Greet thee the Sun,
Greet thee the Moon,
The crops will grow high,
The higher a-soon.

One is the first,
And One is the last,
We pray to the Old Uns,
To make 'em grow fast.

10 Of Calls

The essential purpose of calls is to stir the blood and make it quicken. For without these sonics, which literally thrill, any magical work will lack in potency.

The ancient cries were always sent forth on the wind, from a hill top or other desolate meeting-place of the coven. The invoking calls were given by the leader before the commencement of the rites. They were, in the main, vowel sounds, which were the first sounds people made before learning how to use the lips and tongue for forming words. It has been found that with the use of these very primitive invocations, goose-pimples rise on the skin, and the hairs of one's head literally stand on end. This is evidence of a link between Divine Intelligence and the people concerned.

We must remember that higher intelligences can be contacted through *vibration*, and this is the secret behind the ancient calls.

If they are intoned correctly, with everyone mentally focusing upon the God or Goddess to be invoked, contact will be made and an answering flow of energy returned, the participants feeling it as a peculiar resonance in their vocalization. Once experienced, it will never be forgotten, as the effect is one of exhilaration and upliftment.

This return of energy must be carefully controlled by the leaders of the group, and *they* must be the ones to decide when the exchange has reached the maximum for the group as a whole. Otherwise, the weakest link (person) can prove to be the 'short' in the circuit, and may experience a temporary black-out.

There are one or two different methods which can be used with sonics. A suitable formula must first be decided upon by the coven, and its members must all concentrate upon *where* the sounds are to be directed. The leader can then intone the call, with the rest answering at regular intervals, or alternatively, they may be performed collectively. It is imperative, however, that all present 'feel' the sounds deep within themselves, so that they are calling Inwardly, as well as Outwardly. In other words, we are attempting to raise our own consciousness to a higher level, in order to be heard and answered by Inner Intelligences.

It is important, in all ritual, that the voice be trained, and its tone well formed and modulated. Someone who has a harsh, strident voice, or a squeaky one, is hardly likely to penetrate the correct vibrations of tone to their human group, let alone, Divinity. Yet, if the mind is pure and resolute, there will be a natural improvement of the voice in time, as the mind always affects the body, for good or ill.

Within the structure of the Craft, there are certain well-known, basic calls used by the majority of witches. There are also many that are not so well-known, and, for very good reasons, have been kept secret. A few of the latter will be examined in order to give a general understanding of them, while by no means breaking the secret tradition. It will be understood that most of the calls are used in conjunction with the dances.

I-o-evoe-ee is an ancient call which is still in popular use today. As an invocation it is excellent, and was an important one in ancient Greece, where it was intoned by the priests of the temples. Although witches use it, it seems to be an adaptation of the following: Ieo-veo-veo-veo-veov-orov-ov-

ovovo. Both these calls bring to mind the Yo-heave-ho, of sailors, which may have derived from them. I-o-evoe-ee is used in the present day by the priests of some Hindu temples, but is pronounced evorrrrrr and drawn out, with the tongue touching the roof of the mouth and the lips drawn back.

It is, of course, the pronunciation of the vowels which is important, because all sounds produce sound waves. The calls which follow are very ancient, and have been scientifically examined during the last twenty years. The findings are extraordinary in that some are male, and others female.

Certain calls are only effective when used by many people at once. Others can be powerful if intoned by only one person. As an example, there is one call, Aaahhi-oooo-uuuu, which, if used by a female in an open space, will draw any male walking past and cause him to change direction (or at least have a strong desire to do so), and go in the direction of the call.

This will apply in exactly the same way if a male uses the call I-ee-o-u-e-eeaie, and will draw females. It is not proposed to give the exact pronunciation of these calls; this knowledge must remain, as it always has, in safe hands, within the structure of the Craft. The reason for this is that some of the calls evoke strong sexual feelings, and could, therefore, be used to persuade a person against his or her will.

The following are examples of the soundwaves produced by various calls:

H-U-O-

H-O

125

H-A-A-H-H-I-O-O-U-U

A-A-A-H-H-I-O-O-O-O-U-U-U-U

A-H-A-A-A-R-R-R

The sound I-s-e is really a hissing sound, and is principally a male one. 'Hissing' acts upon the pituitary gland, causing it to produce more adrenalin. It is also a sound always emitted by the male, just before he reaches the climax in sexual intercourse. This is done (perhaps unconsciously) to stimulate the female, who is usually behind the male in reaching orgasm. Just at the point of climax, the man's head often goes to the female's ear. After kissing the mouth of the female, his mouth goes again to the ear of his partner and emits this sound again to stimulate the pituitary gland. It is a basic and primitive noise made only to excite the female.

A sobbing, shrieking, shrilling sound, with pauses, but continually enunciated, will lead to lactation in a nursing mother. But occasionally it has been known to result in lactation in a woman who was not nursing a child at the time. Also, the sound does not necessarily have to be made by a young child, as it is the sound *itself* which creates the effect.

The sounds Eeeeeee and Yee-uu-ee-uu are made by male and female babies, respectively, and the sex of a new-born child can be discerned at birth, by the first cry it utters. If the child is male, the noise will be Eeeeeee. Again, the sound of pleasure emitted by the female at the first climax in sexual intercourse is usually the female Yee-uu-ee-uu, sometimes prolonged.

The pronunciation of the names of the Mother Goddess - Aphrodite, Astarte, etc, were very different in classical and pre-classical times. They would have had great effect on the hearers when the correct intonations were observed.

126

With regard to the secret names of the Goddess, two are given below:

Ororiouth   (Artemis, Selene and Hecate)

Aruru   (Aphrodite)

These have a definite meaning, sometimes of a sexual nature, and within their structure there are both creative and destructive elements. They have a direct link with the forces of Life and Death within them, illustrative of the fact that all acts of creation are also acts of destruction.

During orgasm the man shows, in a lesser degree, all the symptoms of death, and these are present at the time. Further proof is shown by the fact that when a soldier enters the field of battle, knowing that his chances of survival are very small, he will sometimes ejaculate. This is, no doubt, psychological, but has been observed in the cases of condemned men, at the last moment before death, or simultaneously with it. A similar thing occurs in the case of a boy dating a particular girl for the first time. Before the actual meeting, he experiences a mild form of depression; he is not sure, but is hoping that sexual intercourse will take place. Then, after the meeting, the girl gives him some encouragement and he is happier. If the sex act does take place - *ecstasy*. Afterwards, depression may again manifest for a short period.

It has been shown that the ancient calls of the Old Religion are not meaningless sounds (as some writers on the subject reiterate with monotonous regularity), but were made with the intent of stimulating the spiritual and physical natures of the participants. It also appears that the male is the representation of the destructive qualities in Nature, while the female carries the qualities of creation - the precise aspects inherent in the ancient deities, the Horned God and the Mother Goddess!

11 The Mysteries of Symbolism

There are hundreds of magical symbols which have been used throughout the world by various religions, sects, and occult fraternities. Many of them are familiar and have been examined and written about. Symbols such as the Pentagram (five-pointed star); the Star of David (six-pointed star); the Swastika, the Cross and others.

There are, however, many symbols which are not so well-known; they also contain occult secrets within them, but they have been virtually ignored. Whether this is because writers are ignorant of their hidden meanings, or have failed to see any relevance in them, other than a decorative use, remains a mystery. It is proposed, therefore, to look at some of the neglected ones.

The Babylonian Lamp, was, and still is, used as a symbol of the ancient Babylonian goddess, Aruru, later known as Aphrodite. The Lamp is a symbol of fertility, being a representation of the vagina; but when two moths are added (as in the illustration on page 130) it becomes a symbol of blind love and destruction. The two moths, male and female, are attracted by the flame of the Lamp, in which they will eventually perish.

It also symbolizes Life (lamp) and Death (moths). This lamp, called Arura in many languages, warns against attempting any form of sex-magic, without *wisdom* and *instruction*. Aladdin's lamp carries the same message within it.

A very ancient symbol from which the Lamp was probably derived is also illustrated. It is used in many lands as being synonymous with procreation, especially in north-west Australia. In India it is a symbol of destruction and is comparable with the lingam and the yoni.

In certain old scripts the names of Adam and Eve appear written thus:

Adam

Eve

Adam is the phallus, and Eve represents the male and female conjoined.

An old Indian religious sign is:

which may be compared with a sign engraved on a witch knife, or athame:

Although the deeper meanings of these signs obviously cannot be revealed, it will be seen that both of them show the magical power going forth.

Often, on the base of classical statues of the Goddess, just under the feet, was a script written thus:

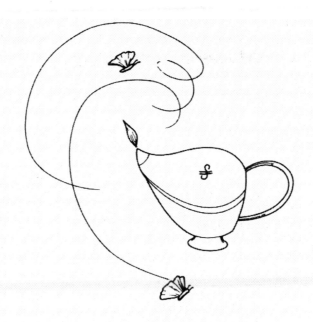

Arura

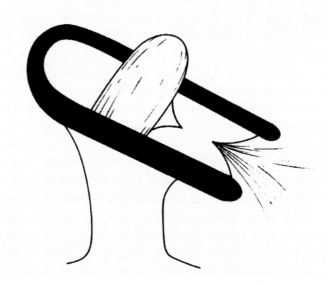

When this script was present, the worshipper was only supposed to look upon the feet of the Goddess, and not at the face. The reason for this now seems apparent if it is compared with the symbol used in some Sex Clinics today:

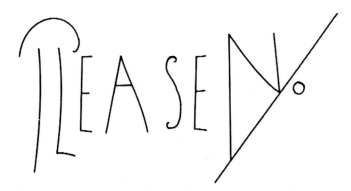

Meditation upon this symbol, from fifteen minutes to half an hour, is said to produce a state of sexual excitement in male or female. It appears that the actual letters are of little importance; it is mainly the form and shape which produces the effect.

We can assume, therefore, that the design at the feet of the Goddess was put there in order to stimulate the worshippers and arouse the life-forces within them. This assumption is strengthened by the fact that some statues were only shown to the populace at certain festivals of the year. The custom is still preserved on the Continent in the present day, when a statue is brought out and paraded before the people. It is usually a Spring Festival - the natural time of year for fertility.

If the Goddess and Her design were indeed displayed with the intention of giving the people a nudge in the area of their sexual activities, we can see that it was a carefully controlled procedure.

Witches have always been associated with the goat. They are said to have ridden these beasts to the Sabbats and there are many pictorial representations of them actually flying through the air on a goat's back.

The goat has also been associated with the Black Arts, the face of the creature being symbolic of Black Magic. But, why the goat, of all the animals in the world? One reason could be the fact that the goat is very lecherous, and this would make it the ideal animal to be connected with the Devil, especially in the eyes of the Christian Church. Even so, there are quite a few animals with this attribute; the stoat for example. Yet, it is always the goat which incurs this doubtful privilege.

The Christian Church has always been very much against the idea of sex for pleasure. Sex for procreation was acceptable, as long as the participants were Catholics, breeding more little Catholics.

To say that the goat is an animal of evil, is ludicrous and yet it has been a constant symbol of evil throughout the whole of the Christian era.

Some Black Magic sects have certainly made the goat the emblem of their practices, as did the Knights Templars with their god Baphomet. Yet, it can be seen that the representation of their deity encompassed all nature in the one symbol and personifies animals by the head of a goat!

The word 'Baphomet' reveals the universal aspects of the figure. When written backwards, we find three abbreviations; TEM, OHP, AB, which in Kabbalistic terms stand for *Templi omnium hominum pacis abbas* (The father of the temple of universal peace among men). However, we must look much further for the solution of 'why the goat?'.

Horned animals were accentuated in ancient religious artforms. Horns were important; they were a symbol of power and majesty, hence the ancient altars were decorated with them. The beautiful horns on the top of the temple at Knossos were carved out of stone and through them one views the Mount of Ida, the home of the gods.

A very early religious concept was the Horned Gate which stood before the entrance to tombs and sacred places in Megalithic times. It also survives at Stonehenge in the lofty trilithons of Sarsen stones standing in horseshoe shape. The way which leads between day and night, life and death, human and divine. Yet, it is the *face* of the goat which is most frequently depicted in witchcraft.

If we look with the eyes of ancient man, who saw pictures in practically everything, we can see the goat's face when a female witch stands in the Pentagram position which is assumed in the ceremonies. Her arms are the horns; her breasts, its eyes; and her pubic hair, its beard (see illustration overleaf). Also, the pubic hair itself in some cases looks like the face of a goat.

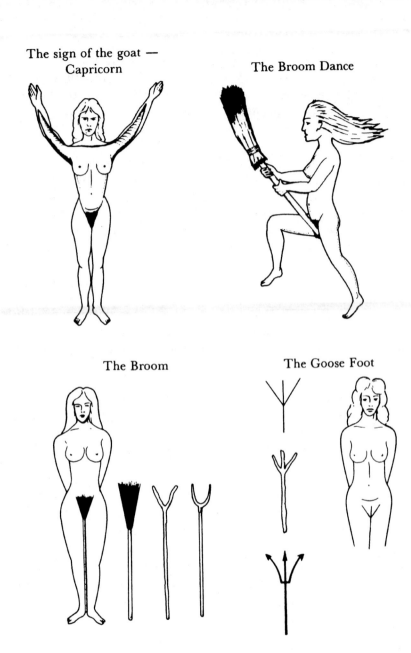

The sign of the goat — Capricorn

The Broom Dance

The Broom

The Goose Foot

By Arnold Crowther

This simple imaginative figure soon became enlarged, especially when the Christian Church started persecuting the Old Religion. Witches, the priestesses of that faith, were depicted with goats between their legs and riding these animals. The goat became an evil character. Devils, demons and most villains were given goatee beards. Expressions such as 'scape-goat' and 'it gets my goat' came from a dislike of the animal.

From these observations it can be understood how witches became so closely associated with the goat, and why, through enforced confessions, often garbled, it was recorded that the goat was synonymous with witchcraft.

The Broom (see illustration) is a well-known symbol of witches and was a later development of the Pole. Due to the persecutions it became necessary to disguise the latter, and the phallic part was hidden in a bundle of twigs. Thus, it became a representation of the Twin Forces of life and the Broom Dance was performed for fertility in the Old Festivals.

'Having a broom between her legs' became a vulgar expression, as did 'She rode a broom', implying sexual intercourse. Today, the word 'ride' is still in use among certain sections of the community when allusions to sex arise. 'Broom' or 'brush' are also common terms for a woman's pubic hair. The broom symbolizes the power of the witch, especially when it is placed upright in the ground; the sign of the Goddess.

Another, though much older goddess symbol, is the 'Goose-foot' (the illustration shows how it was conceived from the shape of a woman). The Trident is also a variation of this symbol. The three prongs represent the most ancient form of Trinity; that of the Goddess, who was known as the Goddess Triformis, or the 'three in one'. Under the names of Diana and Hecate she also held the title of Trivia - 'of the three ways' - and her statues always stood at places where three roads met.

The Stang is a two-pronged forked stick known in Scotland as a 'Bune Wand'. Made from ash wood it is about the height of a man. The witch was usually given one at her initiation, along with a pot of unguent - the famous Flying Ointment. It was upon this staff that the witches did most of their 'flying', most probably due to the mysterious potion. When meetings are held outside, the Stang is placed outside the North of the Circle to represent the God. Sometimes a pitchfork is used as a substitute, but if the ceremony takes place at a time of the year when the Goddess is paramount, the three-pronged staff is used in its stead.

The symbol of the Crook is known in the present day as the Bishop's Crozier. In the Near and Middle East in early times, the Crook was the property of the Great Goddess, when it was known as the 'Crook of Shepherdship'. The Goddess was deeply revered as the one who bestowed the rights of shepherdship and kingship through a matrilineal society. The Crook, together with the Frail, which was carried by the pharaohs, symbolized the pastoral aspects of their rulership over the land.

In occult terms it has been suggested that the Crook, by its shape, shows the power, or energy, rising in man, or woman, from the base of the spine to the head, the seat of the Will. The Crook can also represent a person bowing at the altar of the Goddess.

The Triangle is an ancient symbol of the religion of the Goddess. It was found all over the Middle East and also in Asia and Egypt, incised upon figurines of the Goddess and also placed before tombs and sacred places. The age of the symbol gives a clue to its sanctity. It links directly with the belief of reincarnation as it represented death and re-birth through the Great Goddess. She was known as Nintinugga, 'She who gives life to the Dead', and the 'Mistress of the Mountain of the Dead'. When carved upon a figure of the

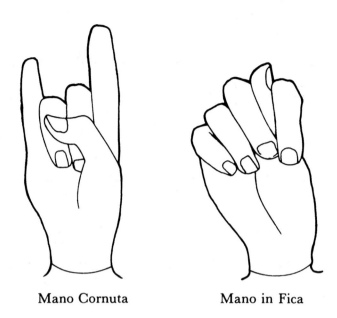

Mano Cornuta   Mano in Fica

By Ian Lilleyman

Goddess, the triangle was in the position, and following the shape of, the pubic hair. It is the downward pointing triangle of the Waters of Life, showing the Gate of birth and re-birth. Further, it symbolizes the Gate of the Mysteries, and the birth of the initiate into the Craft.

Hand signs and signals were common in times gone by. During the persecutions the model of a hand was sometimes placed in a cottage window. If the back of the hand faced the person outside, it meant that it was safe to enter; it beckoned one in. But, if the palm was turned to the window, the signal implied, 'keep out! It is not safe'.

Two hand signs, which were also used by witches, were the *Mano Cornuta* and the *Mano in Fica*. The first one, 'making horns', was to avert the Evil Eye. It was achieved by holding up the first and the little finger of the hand; the other two fingers being held down by the thumb. The gesture symbolizes the power and protection of the Horned God.

The *Mano in Fica*, or 'the fig', was a feminine sign representing the Goddess and the clitoris. It was made by clenching the fist and pushing the thumb up between the first and second fingers. 'The fig' was sometimes employed to keep away evil though it was generally used as a blessing. Witches still retain it as a sign of recognition between each other.

The art of symbolism is a very ancient one and was used to perpetuate religious or occult secrets and beliefs. In this way they have been preserved, safe from vulgar cupidities, yet available to those souls who truly *will* to unravel, uphold and practise, the Secrets of the Holy Mysteries.

12 Methods of Divination

Ways of Divination are many and varied and most of the conventional ones have received attention in other books. There are, however, some methods which have been handed down to me and which I have found to be effective, especially within the framework of the Craft.

The first of these is the Mirror working. Ideally, all magic circles should have a speculum, in the form of an ordinary glass mirror, hanging on the wall which aligns most closely to the magnetic North. The mirror should be large enough to reflect the altar, if not most of the Circle. It should first be consecrated, then covered with a black velvet, or silver curtain when not in use. The curtain can be embroidered with the magical sigils of the Moon, which may be echoed around the mirror itself.

It will be realized that all workings of this kind link with the Astral Plane of which the Moon is the ruler. The mirror is of utmost importance in the building of the Astral Temple, which is a duplicate of the material temple and a vital necessity in some works of magic. The Astral Temple is visualized and built up by the imagination, and will be real in its own sphere as long as it is used in this way.

It is especially useful to dwell in the Astral Temple during meditation. Its furnishings must be as familiar as those of the physical one, and should be used in the same manner. However, its structure should be kept most secret and within the coven who makes it, so that it remains inviolate from any other minds.

For individual workings with the Magic Mirror, I will give details of methods which link with the four elements: Air, Fire, Water and Earth. And it is assumed that the Circle has been consecrated and made ready. The following rituals can be worked sky-clad, or robed, as the practitioner prefers.

Aír

This method is ideal for single ideas or things you wish to occur or come to pass; to send telepathic messages to friends, or to receive an answer to a problem.

Take up your athame and draw an invoking pentagram in front of the mirror. Then sit comfortably, holding your athame upright in your hand, which may rest on your knee. Have one pale yellow candle lit and placed where it suits you best.

Now, you have examined the idea and found that in no way will be harm anyone that it is not something impossible or utterly beyond your reach, and that there is no reason why it should not be granted.

Take five deep breaths, close your eyes, and begin to visualize the idea happening in your mind. Take your time and hold the thought for as long as you feel is necessary. Then open your eyes and visualize your thought in the mirror. See it clearly, and hold the image a while; and now begin to intone the idea in actual words. Speak softly and clearly, and to the point. Repeat the words seven times, then lift up your athame and stab the point towards the mirror, seven times.

Now release the image, clear it from your mind and let it go into the beyond to do its work. Dismiss it from your mind completely, because it cannot do its work while you hold on to it. Relax; take five deep breaths as if to blow the idea into the Astral. Empty your mind and think of nothing, or no-thing. For a few minutes become a vacuum, or as a leaf that is blown about in the air. Then rise up with the feeling that all is well, and without doubts or scepticism.

You may leave the candle alight in a safe place, or keep it to use again in the same ritual, for the same reasons, but for no other.

Fire

This method is useful in training the mind to visualize colours, and to activate or develop a physical attribute which is lacking, or is not strong enough in the practitioner.

Take up the wand and draw an invoking pentagram in front of the mirror. Place a red candle, about four inches, before the mirror, with its flame in the centre of the pentagram. Hold up the wand, so it can rest upon your knee, and concentrate upon the flame in the mirror until you begin to see an aura around it. This will be about four inches in diameter and composed of various colours like the rainbow; it may be oval in shape, or like a halo or a circle.

After a few minutes the aura will increase in size, with a few bright rays seeming to come from the flame directly towards you. If you see these rays, you will know that you are succeeding, and that your powers of concentration are good.

Now, take your eyes away from the frame and look only at the aura. Say to yourself, 'Blue-blue-blue.......' and repeat this seven times.

In a while you should find the aura is changing to a beautiful blue colour, and while this is manifesting begin to feel yourself bathed in this colour. Imagine it all around you and part of you, then start to feel yourself developing one of the attributes associated with this shade.

Then try the same procedure with another colour, such as green or red. If a particular attribute is required, the whole ritual may be devoted to the colour which links with it. The following is a list of colours and their influences:

Red — Courage; strength; enthusiasm; passion; belief; work; drive.

Orange — Confidence; hope; health; optimism; cheerfulness.

Yellow — Alertness; memory; eloquence; effort; tolerance; wit.

Green — Generousness; honesty; firmness; reflection; responsibility.

Blue — Benevolence; independence; graciousness; happiness; devotion; forgiveness.

Violet — Clairvoyance; vision; spirituality; patience; calmness; prudence; sympathy; persistence.

White — Compassion; illumination; discernment; inspiration.

Water

Here we have the natural element which links with the Astral Plane, memory, past lives and those to come.

Have two horn cups, or goblets, one empty, one filled with water. Light a blue candle and place it beneath the mirror. Dip the first finger into the water and draw a pentagram in

142

front of the mirror, touching the glass at each point of the symbol.

Now take up the two vessels and begin pouring the water slowly, from one to the other. The sound should make you feel very calm and peaceful. As you pour, repeat the following words:

> *Ebb and flow; ebb and flow;*
> *Show me the things that I should know.*
> *Past and present; future too;*
> *Who have I been; and what will I do?*
> *Silvery water; silvery Moon;*
> *Give me an answer to this little rune.*
>   *'So mote it be!'*

Then put the empty vessel on the ground and hold the full one on your lap: Relax your body and mind. Sit quietly and gaze calmly at your reflection. Do not stare intently, or try to force things to happen. This would ensure that they didn't!

Imagine you are in a deep pool, floating gently on the water. After a while, the mirror will darken and your face will disappear. This is a sign that your eyes are beginning to tire, and quite usual in these circumstances. But this is when the Third Eye will begin to take over, and you may see a face other than your own in the glass. You may also feel different emotions surging within you, which belong to that other face. This may please or displease you. You may even see whole episodes from a previous life. These will have been evoked from your subconscious mind and may give you a clue as to what sort of person you were in the past. Also, why you had to be re-born. This experience may only happen once in your life, but if it does you will remember it always.

When the vision fades, it is time to conclude the experiment and leave it for another day. Take in some deep breaths and return gradually to your ordinary surroundings. Sit a few minutes longer; drink the water, which has become pranarized, or oxygenized, through the constant pouring from one vessel to the other. Say a few words of thanks to the Old Ones, and replace the curtain over the mirror.

Earth

This meditation is good for the building-up of the life-force, especially if you have been ill, or lack energy in any way. You are going to evoke the Earth spirit.

Have a green candle burning, and place it in front of the mirror. Take up the pentacle and hold it up to the glass; saying:

> *Spirit of Life; spirit of Earth;*
> *By Magic I call you, in the name of my birth!*
> *Fill me with health, as your herbs in the Sun;*
> *By Pentacle bright, may the Magic be done!*
> *'So Mote it be.'*

Now, place the pentacle on your breast; make sure it is still the right way up; and see its reflection through the mirror. Gaze at it for a while, then pick up the candle in your other hand and hold it so that the flame is in the centre of the pentacle.

Begin to visualize the pentacle as what it is, a creature of the earth, and attune your mind to Mother Nature. Look at it, gleaming and reflecting the candle flame; and in a little while you will see it as field of golden corn, with the flame as the Sun. Other beautiful scenes will unfold before your eyes. In some it will seem as if the pentacle is lying in a garden of flowers, or shining in the midst of a dark forest. But whatever you see, imagine that you are part of it and are benefiting from the powers of the Earth.

At the end, put down the candle; kiss the pentacle, and thank the Gods.

One day some years ago, an old gypsy came to my house. She begged me to try and find for her a glass ball, which she could use as a crystal, for scrying, as her own had been stolen. I said I would have a look, and told her to come back in a few days' time.

My husband said one couldn't give expensive things away to strangers; even glass balls cost quite a lot. But he eventually found a small one in a drawer, and said I could give it to her if she came back.

On her return, I presented the ball to her, and her eyes nearly popped out of her head.

'Can you give me something in return?' I asked.

She looked at me hard, and said, 'You, too, have the sight. Do you understand the cards?'

'Yes,' I said, 'I have studied them for many years.'

'Then listen to me, lovey; I'll tell you an old gypsy way of reading them, which not many gorgios know (Gorgios are white people, who live in houses!) 'But, you must only do it to know something real important like.'

'I understand,' I nodded.

'Have you a cup of tea to spare?' she asked, grinning toothlessly.

'Of course; come into the kitchen and I'll make you one.'

She came in and made herself at home while I brewed the tea.

'You know about the cards being like the elements, don't you?' she asked. I nodded.

'Well, lookee, 'ere; there's a saying among our folk that the shuffling of the cards is the earth; the pattering of the cards is the rain; the beating of the cards is the wind, and the pointing of the cards is the fire'. She pointed a grimy finger at the hearth.

'See? Earth, water, fire and air; see?'

'Ah-ha,' I thought, 'what have we here?' as I placed her tea some home-made scones on the table.

'Bless you, you'll never want,' she said, as she tucked in. I took that with a pinch of salt, as it was something gypsies always said when you bought anything from them.

I waited until she had finished eating, then said, 'Please tell me more'. She dived into her torn coat and pulled out a grubby pack of Tarot cards.

'Now then; see 'ere; this is the way to treat 'em, like a babby'. She pushed away the crockery and put them on the table.

''ave you got a fag?' I gave her one and lit it for her.

'Now, it's this way; earth, water, air and fire, that's what they are, and you must treat 'em like it, so watch me....... ' She began shuffling them.

'This, you see, is the earth; like you turn it over with a spade.' Then she gathered them up and dropped them one after the other, on to the table. 'This is the rain, dropping on the ground.'

She gathered them up again into two packs and beat one pack softly against the other, 'This is the wind, dearie,' she grinned.

Then she spread them out, like a fan, and pointed them to the fire, which gleamed upon their surfaces.

'That's them pointed like the flames,' she said.

'That's really wonderful', I said. 'You are really bringing out their hidden life by doing that.'

'Yes, yes, lovey, but you must do it over and over again, until the elements are part of you, as well as the cards. Then, it is time to read them, and only then.'

Needless to say, I asked her to read the cards for me, before she left.

Divination by the use of rune stones is another way of foretelling the future, and one that has not received much attention in the past by writers on the occult.

Lithomancy, as it is called, is a very primitive method and it is particularly associated with witches; probably because stones were the most convenient things to use in the remote past. But the practice of sortilege, meaning the casting of sorts or lots, to foretell the future, gave the French their word for 'witch', in *sorcier* (male witch) and *sorcière* (female witch). The method I am going to describe, concerns the use of stones, or pebbles, each marked with a different symbol.

The Rune Stones are eight in number, eight being the number of the Craft, and they should be roughly about one inch, or a little less, in diameter. Suitable stones for this type of divination can be collected from the beach, or even an old quarry, though, personally, I think you have a much wider choice on the sea-shore.

When you have studied the stones and their meanings, you will be able to select eight stones which appeal to you for the required reasons.

The symbols can be painted on them in appropriate colours with enamel paint and a fine brush. For example, the Sun stone symbol would be best painted in gold; the Moon stone, silver or white; the Ring stone, pink; the Crossed Spears, red; the Curling Wave stone, blue; the Three Birds stones, red, white and blue, the Lucky stone, yellow; and the symbol on the Black stone painted white; otherwise it will not show up.

The Key to the Rune Stones

 Rune stones marked with a rayed sun. This rune represents any man, or a favourable omen of success. Also, all forms of expansion in life. When this is the leading rune, it forecasts a successful outcome of the matter enquired about. This is the rune of the Sun; it represents honours, fame, and a successful year ahead when it is the *leading* stone.

 Crescent Moon, marked with four splats, indicating the Moon's phases. This stone in the leading position relates to any woman in a question, or wives, childbirth or conception, if that is the matter enquired about. It also forecasts changes in position, due to happen with twenty-eight days, if the stone is in the leading position. It often denotes a visit abroad. The true meaning of the rune can be arrived at by studying the rune that is *nearest* to it in a cast. If the nearest stone is favourable, the coming changes will be favourable.

Rune stone marked with interlocking rings. This has to do with the successful outcome of all *love* and *marriage* questions. When it is the leading rune, it denotes a speedy engagement, marriage, or successful love affair. When *leading*, it is affirmative to the question: 'Does he (or she) love me?'

Rune with crossed spears. When this is the leading rune, it signifies *strife* and *quarrels*. It also stands for a sudden occurrence of an upsetting nature. Often it represents some person who has, or will, quarrel with the enquirer. If a member of the armed forces is the enquired, it could mean sudden promotion. If it lies next to a *fortunate* stone it means the *healing* of a quarrel. If it comes up with the *Love* stone, it means the healing of a romance that has broken off, or a revived romance. For health questions this rune denotes a swift recovery after illness or accident.

Rune stone with curling wave design. This stands for *relatives*, their affairs, and the effect the affairs of kinfolk have on their enquirer. When near the *Sun* stone it forecasts a *long journey*, often abroad, for the enquirer. Near the *Moon* stone it presages a journey for a *relative*. When it lies near to the *Love* stone, it forecasts a romance that could take the enquirer abroad.

Rune with three birds in flight. It represents *sudden news* of an unexpected nature. If a *leading* rune, it could change the whole of one's life, often for the better. Whether leading or not, when it lies with *fortunate* stones, it symbolizes documents or writings that bring joy, also good news from *distant* friends and associates.

This is a *Lucky* stone, representing an 'ear of corn', the sign of plenty. As a leading stone this is the luckiest stone of all, denoting a happy and prosperous outcome of the matter enquired about. It presages the expansion of all things, money, luck, social advancement, and a time of prosperity. Lying with the <u>Love</u> stone it signifies a wealthy marriage! With the *Sun* stone, a brilliant career. With the *Wave* stone, success in distant countries.

A *Black* rune stone cut like an H. When the *leading* stone, it denotes losses, grief, and misfortunes in general, partings, and sometimes bereavements. *It should never be read alone, unless* it is the *only* stone in the cast with a *symbol showing*. The stones lying *near* to it should be read, for these often mitigate what at first looks to be misfortune. For instance, if this stone lies with the *Moon* stone, it would indicate unhappiness that would change within twenty-eight days to something better.

How to Cast the Rune Stones

Take the eight stones in your right hand; shake them up like dice, while thinking of the question you wish to ask, then cast the Runes away from you.

Only the Runes that have the *symbols uppermost* should be read. The ones that fall *face downward* are *out* and have *no meaning*. The Rune stone farthest away from you is the leading stone and the most important. The others *decrease* in importance as they fall *nearer* to you.

150

Only the stones that show a *symbol* have any meaning. If one falls on top of another and *both* show a symbol, those *two* stones carry the answer.

Keep your questions simple; if you ask one and cast and no symbols show, this indicates that the time is not right. *Do not cast again for seven days.*

Never cast the Runes for fun, or if you *know* the *answer*; remember they are an ancient form of divination and *not* a game.

When casting the runes for yourself, *you* are the enquirer; when casting for another, let *them* throw the stones but *you* read them.

To cast the Runes for someone *not present*, concentrate on their problem, then cast and read the stones as if *you* were the enquirer.

Don't try to complicate your readings by asking nebulous questions such as, 'Shall I be happy?'; but rather, 'If I do so and so, will it bring me happiness?' Remember, the Runes are as old as time, so do not expect that you will be able to find a 'long story' at first. Concentrate on simple questions to begin with, and you will soon find that they will tell you their own story in their own way.

Never lend your Runes to another person, because if you do, they will *never again tell a true story*. Remember, they were ritualized for *you alone*.

Finally, keep your Runes in a little velvet or suede bag, which can be embroidered with your magical name, in one of the magical alphabets, or a sigil which is pleasing or powerful to you.

13 Introduction to the Planetary Rituals

The Planetary Rituals have been written principally for members of the Wicca, although in essence they are universal and can be adapted for use by most magical societies.

The main purpose of these rites is to evoke and invoke the various qualities and attributes with which the seven major planets are associated. The Sun and the Moon are luminaries and are known by astrologers as the Two Lights; but they are here named as planets for the sake of convenience.

These archetypal forces, which emanate from the Divine and permeate the universe, have throughout the ages been thought of as gods and goddesses, and, as such, are distinguishable in the material world. In this respect, their influences are the more easily grasped.

This is not to say that such divine beings, by which the planets are named, do not exist. There are thousands of divisions and subdivisions from the One incomprehensible Godhead; as many levels in spiritual worlds as there are in the material or physical world, all issuing from the same Supreme Source of Origin.

As most occultists know, an invocation to any of the Gods, if properly performed, can result in the appearance of that Godform. They are most often seen clairvoyantly, and in the most exquisite colours, quite unlike those of the physical world, which seem drab in comparison.

The Seven Planets have their correspondences in every kind of manifestation. Their influences penetrate plants, trees, colours, metals, minerals, jewels, animals, birds, humans, and even time, in the days of the week and the hours in a day.

The performance of a Planetary Rite is to avoid the 'cold' start in magical work, though they can also be performed as a rite in themselves, or as a complement to a particular festival.

The most important thing, in all works of magic, is to be in the correct frame of mind, and to feel the correct emotions surging within you. Even the strongest will-power and concentration upon a desired result will fail without this Inner arousal.

For adepts and experienced witches, this condition may be easily and quickly acquired, but for the many newcomers, at various stages of development, it can be extremely difficult.

All genuine groups consist of members at different levels of advancement, and progressing in the degrees. No doubt, as in ancient times, there are meetings of the coven to which only those in the higher grades are admitted. When the full coven meets, however, all the witches are required to work, as far as possible, in unison.

If the meeting is arranged for the performance of magical work, as opposed to a celebration or a festival, the work is usually initiated soon after the traditional opening of the Circle. This is where the Planetary Rites are of value. For example, if the work concerns illness, then the Rite of the Sun would precede the actual healing session. The exception here would be that if it were a nervous disorder, the Rite of Mercury would be used.

All the witches, therefore, have time during the rite to attune themselves, by invocation of the God or Goddess of the rite, and by evocation of the rays of healing from within themselves. So that when the actual work takes place, these necessities are already present and ready to use.

The purpose of any ritual is to produce within the participants a thrilling of their astral bodies, which should vibrate through the whole being, the words and actions strongly moving and stimulating the people involved.

Some witches become bored through repetition of certain rituals; they fail to exhilarate, so naturally, fail to produce the required effects. If this is so, then it is very important to confide in the leaders of the coven.

Nothing connected with the Craft remains static. The symbol of the Circle is *movement*. A well-run coven is one which anticipates *change*. This means that the people in charge have knowledge to impart and are willing to teach it.

A coven which has the same members for many years may be very strong and proficient, yet lacking in other ways, and surely in danger of stagnation. In such a coven there must be those who have the necessary qualifications to initiate a new group, thus making way for newcomers.

All orders, magical or otherwise, need new blood from time to time, and the Craft is no exception. Even during the period of the persecutions, people were brought in. 'Conceal the Mysteries; reveal them constantly,' is an axiom of the Old Religion.

Fare-well!

14 The Rite of Saturn

Day	Saturday
Incense or	Hyacinth; pansy; pepperwort; asafoetida;
perfume	Black poppy seeds, henbane; lodestone; myrrh.
Wood	Oak
Colour	Black or Indigo.
Influences	Duties; responsibilities; finding familiars; works of Magic; buildings; meditation; life; death; doctrines.

Son of Cronos; Father of the Gods; the God of Time; the Silent Watcher; the One Alone; the Wise One. Linking in the Tarot with the World, which is the place of our initiation, through life's trials and sorrows.

Saturn has been described as the Taskmaster of the Zodiac, because he gives the lessons to be learned in life. Wherever Saturn is placed in a natal chart will show the kind of lesson prepared for the native, thus giving an opportunity to acquaint oneself with the direction from which certain of life's vicissitudes will stem, and being to the native's advantage.

Saturn is the ruler of Capricornus the Goat, and anyone born under this sign usually finds that he gives his favours after middle age. Saturn being in rapport with experience and the 'not so young'.

The reasons for this ritual should be those of a sombre nature: quietness, but alertness of the Inner Mind; contemplation and penetration of the psychic realms; long-term ambitions to bring fruition at a future time.

The Rite begins in complete darkness. The witches should stand in absolute silence and calmness for as long as is deemed necessary. The mind must be freed from all extraneous thoughts and allowed to meditate on the unmanifest, or no-thing. When ready, the Server (or Maiden), lights one *black* candle on the altar, and eyes should be focused just above its flame. Very slowly, adjust the thoughts to the reason and purpose of the rite. Not intensely; rather in a dreamy faraway manner, as though looking at the idea from a long distance. The members now link hands; still keeping the calm of the atmosphere.

HIGH PRIESTESS

We who look upon the flame of inspiration, remember well its origins. Out of the Womb of Time is it born, as an innocent babe, virginal and pure. Let us, therefore, think deeply of our intent and keep it in like manner, free from all undesirable thoughts or pollution of any kind.

The Server now lights the candles at the four gates, from the central one, and the Circle is erected in the usual manner.

HIGH PRIEST

I am He before who life itself was created; from whom light was brought forth from darkness - the Great Mother. Consider well thy purpose, that it is worthy to be brought into manifestation.

The High Priestess whispers the purpose of the rite to the person on her left. It is thus passed round the Circle, and the last person to receive it gives it to the High Priest.

HIGH PRIEST
It is - that it is!

He raises the Wand and points it to the North; at the same time reaffirming the intent, *aloud.*

ALL
Give us the true intent of mind, to bring our wish to birth.

High Priest stands in God position.
The witches must see the High Priest as the God now, and he must identify with the God, himself.

HIGH PRIESTESS
O! Thou who art all and nil; give us the wisdom to discover our true path in this incarnation. May we dwell long in the darkness of our minds; considering all our faults and also our true wills.

The 'Dance of the Lame God' is now performed. While this is in progress, any of the witches may go forward to the 'God' and whisper to him their chief fault, asking him for guidance to correct it. As the person goes forward, the others immediately link hands again, keeping the Circle in formation. The following chant is suitable, being simple, effective and allowing freedom of mind.

ALL
'*Ee-evoe-ee*' (pronounced slowly and softly)

While approaching the 'God', any person may offer a lighted candle, or give any token to symbolize faith and trust.

The Dance should not be limited to time, but when ready the High Priest should give a prearranged signal for the dance to cease.

If trance occurs in any person, the High Priestess should attend, the dance continuing with chant muted.

At end, all stand in complete silence, while the High Priest takes up a lighted lantern, and the stang or pole. He then proceeds with them round the Circle, three times, after which he presents them to each witch in turn, who does likewise. The last person, returns the lantern and stang to him. While thus employed, the witch should meditate on all the aspects of Saturn; wisdom, old age, time, death, winter, etc.

MAGICAL WORK NOW TAKES PLACE, IF WILLED.

Server sounds the Horn, to signify attention from Inner to Outer reality.

HIGH PRIESTESS
We have a long path to tread, but we trust in Thee and time, to bring us to our true fulfilment. To make us wise and patient; awaiting our potentiality in Cosmos.

HIGH PRIEST
Why wait? The time is always - *Now!*

All circle slowly with linked hands, to the following chant:

ALL
Take our wish and give it birth;
Thou who dwells in darkest earth;
Time and tide will all unite;
To give it birth, if it is right!

Hear our prayer, O! dreaded God;
By Thy flame and righteous rod;
Hear Thy children here below;
Grant our will and mercy show.
So mote it be!

Females give the fivefold salute to the High Priest, males bow

(It is suggested that the above ritual be performed during the Tide of Recession.)

15 The Rite of Jupiter

Day	Thursday.
Incense or perfume	Stock; lilac; storax; aloes; nutmeg; henbane.
Wood	Pine
Colour	Purple.
Influences	Luck; religion; trade and employment; treasure; honours; riches; legal matters

The Great Benefic. Thus is Jupiter named by astrologers. The name is a Latin variant for Zeus.

The position of this planet in the natal chart is one of the most important of the aspects. Whichever house he rules at birth, there will be found fortune. Jupiter links with No 10 in the Tarot; the Wheel of Fortune.

The mood of this Rite should be one of *confidence* and *hope*.

The Circle is first erected in the usual manner. The witches then stand round it with arms akimbo. At the signal of a shake from tambarine or sistrum, all greet one another, exchanging banter, kisses, and exuding a friendly *bon-ami*. The atmosphere must be well charged with happiness and good comradeship.

The Server fills for horned cup with wine and gives it to the High Priestess, who raises it above the altar.

HIGH PRIEST
Great is Jupiter; grant that He will give us good luck!

All repeat this toast.

High Priestess passes the Cup round, and all imbibe freely. She then replaces it upon the altar.

HIGH PRIESTESS
Pleasure be ours. Pleasure be to all who dwell under the Gods. Know ye all this, if work be well done and enjoyed, pleasure and happiness will be thrice the reward. Then be at peace. Enjoy the gifts which bounteous Jupiter bestows on thee.

Here, music of a cheerful nature is played, either by a member of the group or relayed on a tape-recorder. The witches dance *as they will*.

At the end the High Priest claps his hands for order.

HIGH PRIEST
Now is Jupiter dwelling among us. Let us give Him due homage.

All kneel on one knee.

ALL
We hail Thee great Jupiter. *Well-come!*

All rise.

HIGH PRIESTESS
O! Thou great One who gives joy to mankind; we praise Thee, and trust that by our rite Thou wilt be well satisfied.

ALL
So mote it be!

Circle Dance to a suitable chant now takes place. This should be as light-hearted as possible, with an occasional leap into the air.

HIGH PRIEST and HIGH PRIESTESS

Now, good people all; let us call our highest hopes to Him - the Jovial One of All. May our hopes by all fulfilled. If not today; in future - *willed. Hurraya*!

ALL
Hurraya!

HIGH PRIESTESS
Let us now consider the object of our rite. Can we truly say that we are as happy as we ought to be? Consider well this incarnation which was given to us. If we believe in the Old Ones, we should try to understand that our journey is most carefully protected. We have our own wills but may not be using them for the right purposes. We should not sorrow too long over past mistakes or lost loved ones. They would not wish it - and we who know but little of the Mystery of Life are not the right ones to judge it. So, Merry Meet and Merry Part; think on the Craft's old saying. Lift up the horseshoe and also thy heart; tis but a game that we're playing.

High Priest raises the horseshoe, then lowers it between the Altar candles and holds position. He then gives it to the High Priestess who kisses it and hands it round the Circle.

HIGH PRIESTESS
Good luck, great joy to all say I. May this hold thy luck for aye.

Each person takes it and holds it up, mentally making his or her own particular wish. On its return, the High Priestess

161

hands it to the High Priest who places it in the centre of the altar, horns *upwards*.

THE PERFORMANCE OF MAGICAL WORK NOW TAKES PLACE.

Closing

High Priest holds up the horseshoe, while all join hands and circle to the following chant:

ALL
Jupiter, God of the rainbow sky;
Grant our wishes by and by;
Let Thy blessings on us shine;
By Horseshoe, Pin, and Finger sign.

Four-leafed Clover, Thou must show;
To bring us luck where ere we go;
Black Cats, Cuckoos, New Moon too;
Aid us now in all we do.
Hail!
(Repeat chant *three* times)

16 The Rite of Mars

Day	Tuesday.
Incense or perfume	Hellebore; carnation; patchouli; lignum aloes; plantain.
Wood	Cedar.
Colour	Red.
Influences	Courage; surgery; physical strength; opposition; war; defence; endurance.

This rite is principally aligned with courage and strength. Not only physical strength, but what is usually required from time to time by all of us; strength of spirit. Mars links with No 16 in the Tarot; the Tower.

The symbolism here is much and varied. In its spiritual aspect, the Tower denotes the human soul coming face to face with the light of God. The result can be illumination or total destruction. It is, therefore, dependent on the individual's intention, and informs us that any student of the Mysteries should be properly prepared before embarking upon the Inner Planes. If there is no sound basis upon which to grow spiritually, the penalty is very plain. Here, the soul is in direct contact with the full glare of divine consciousness. The goal of the mystic quest.

The Circle is opened in the usual manner.

At the beginning of the rite, all are seated cross-legged on the floor. The arms are crossed over the chest with the hands clenched. The breathing should be deep and rhythmical; the mind concentrating upon cosmic energy, in whatever form the

163

individual best feels a rapport. Stars and planets being born and rushing through space. Mars itself, or a symbol of power such as the Cerne Giant. Remember it is the *influence* of Mars we are trying to evoke.

A gong stroke signifies termination of meditation.

The witches rise slowly to their feet, unfolding their arms and unclenching their hands. Raising their arms into an upward V position, they link hands and begin to move round the Circle in a sideways movement. With one step at a time, a rhythm should be kept by stamping the left foot on the ground.

At some point during the above circling, the High Priest goes up to the altar, where he dons the horned helmet. At a given signal by him, of three stamps on the ground, the members come to a halt.

HIGH PRIEST
Be thou all of true heart?

ALL
Yea!

HIGH PRIEST
Be thou all of true will?

ALL
Yea!

HIGH PRIEST
Be thou sound in wind and limb?

ALL
Yea!

HIGH PRIEST

Then fear nought under the Heavens but the High Gods.
(One stroke on gong)

HIGH PRIEST
By the power of Earth; by the power of Mind; by the power of Body; by the power of Mars; may we be endowed. Lift up the Staff of Life; that by this symbol we can see, the strength that governs all of We.

High Priestess raises the stang (or pole), and passes it round the Circle. While holding it, each person evokes the utmost feelings of strength and energy that they are capable of manifesting. The symbol is then returned to the High Priestess, who gives it to the High Priest.

HIGH PRIEST
Grasp ye the symbol of strength and joy and give it due recognition. Circle around in the Wheel of Life, with fortitude and ambition.

All circle slowly with a marching step, right hand holding the stang, left hand on the shoulder of the person in front. (Alternate male and female, if possible)

ALL
Round this symbol we do tread;
Fearing nought that lies ahead;
Courage in us brightly burns;
As this wheel of witches turns.

One by one around we go,
Straight of back from top to toe;
Flame of courage burning bright,
On our way into the light.

As we tread the measure proud,
One and all we shout aloud;

Make us as this Rod so high
Balanced twix't the Earth and Sky.
(Repeat three times)

High Priestess now takes the stang and holds it in a horizontal position, while the witches stand quietly in a circle.

HIGH PRIESTESS
Even as this Rod is balanced in perfection, so may our judgement in all matters be likewise, not wanting in weight or measure. Not favouring one side more than the other. To attain this perfect poise, we must search deep within our hearts. With unclouded and unprejudiced minds, we must strive to see clearly and objectively, and indeed fairly, all wrongs which are brought to our notice, or disputes which may arise among us. The Scales of Justice balance in the wind. The verdict must be just. Our souls must weigh against the Feather of Truth.
(Replaces stang upon the altar)

Guilt should not be left to weigh down the soul in the quagmire of despair. Guilt must be dug out of its dark hiding-place and brought quaking, into the bright silver streak of the noble Sword. Cut off from its feed of envy or hate, let it perish swiftly, in one clean stroke.

High Priest raises the sword and brings it down to the ground in a sweeping curve.

HIGH PRIESTESS
Now, the soul be free again, seeing with clear eyes, its follies and mistakes. Thus, and thus only, is the way of justice and strength, in the Craft.
So mote it be!

ALL
So mote it be!

166

(Replace sword on altar)

HIGH PRIESTESS
Lightly now, springs the soul again, with new hope and joy.
The tears of contrition heal the wounds which have beset it.
The child, once more, made whole. Blessed be!

ALL
Blessed be!

HIGH PRIEST
The great test of Mars is always strength. Not only of body,
but also of soul. In every kind of affliction, mental or physical,
Mars is the most terrible of all our initiations. As of old,
likewise today. The terrors and tests set for all true initiates
can only be overcome by courage; fierceness by gentleness,
anger by honesty, rage by sweetness. The Lion of lust and
carnality can only be tamed by the power of the mind. Real
love is the meeting of two souls and thus only can a true
union be achieved. The Lion then becomes a winged animal in
this, the highest concept of Love. Such a union can be the
Gate of re-birth for an 'old' soul.

THE PERFORMANCE OF MAGICAL WORK

Closing

All circle slowly with *majestic* step to the following:

ALL
Consecrate our souls this night;
Fill us now with sweetest light;
Purge our passions with Thy gold;
So we may the Gods behold.

Circle all with lightened step,
That our terrors shall be met;

Swiftly calmed and strongly healed
As the warrior in the field.

(Repeat *three* times)

High Priest lifts up the sword and the High Priestess raises
the crown. High Priestess slowly lowers the crown upon the
uplifted sword.

ALL
Hail to thee O! Sword of Steel;
With thee our errors we do seal;
Crowned by thy silver blade;
Our wrath subdued, our terrors laid.

17 The Rite of the Sun

Day	Sunday.
Incense or perfume	Heliotrope; orange blossom; cloves; frankincense; ambergris; musk; mastic; paliginia; sunflower oil.
Wood	Laurel.
Colour	Orange or Gold.
Influences	Health; healing; confidence; hope; prosperity; vitality.

The Rite of the Sun is a most joyous one. It links with success in all undertakings. It can be performed when a ray of spiritual light is needed, or when energy is required upon a physical level. The Tarot card depicting the Sun shows two children playing and laughing together in their own private, magical world.

In all traditions of the Mysteries, the tenet that, 'ye must be as little children', is one of the most important. Strip away the layers of convention, artificiality, so-called respectability, and everything which divorces the soul from its true potentiality and divinity. Children are not imbeciles; neither are they in any way inferior to their elders. True, their minds are not fully developed, yet neither are they cluttered or closed by the social structure of the Establishment. The real meaning of this mystery is to be 'Truly Free', both in mind and body, and wholly innocent.

In this rite, a fire of some sort should be ready to light in the Circle. One of the safest places, indoors, is within a cauldron or similar receptacle. There can be a round tin inside the cauldron, in which a coil of asbestos twine is placed. A small amount of methylated spirit poured onto the twine will create a very good flame, with no smoke and very little smell.

Erect the Circle

HIGH PRIESTESS
The Rite of the Sun is about to start;
Awake from sleep and take thy part;
Gold and Glory shall be thyne;
As on ye all, his light will shine.

Follow me and tread the Maze;
As was done in olden days;
God and Goddess here come we;
Seeking the ancient Mystery.

As the pattern here below;
Shows us the way we have to go;
Through the Gate of Horn come we;
The rulers of our destiny!

The High Priestess leads the Maze Dance, which may be performed in a spiral pattern. She leads the dancers round the circle; doubling back from time to time, until the centre is reached; where stands the cauldron.

High Priestess takes a taper and lights the cauldron fire from the altar candle.

HIGH PRIESTESS
Take this flame and may it be;
With all of ye - *eternally!*
See how the flame burns bright;
Feel how our hearts unite;
Great is the light of the Sun;

Uniting us as One.
Come!

One by one the witches approach the High Priestess, proceeding deosil. She gives each one a candle which they light from the cauldron fire. The females are also presented with a garland of flowers, which she places upon their heads. (If this is not possible, they are given a single flower to wear in their hair.)

High Priest raises wand above cauldron and invokes:

HIGH PRIEST
We invoke Thee O Lord of Light, giver of Life and Fertility. Thy children encircle this fire, as our Earth and planets encircle Thee; receiving Thy blessed warmth and miraculous rays.

Oh, Great One - symbol of the Supreme, Masculine Force of Life, Thy golden light shines on the faces of Thy children, as we marvel at Thy enormous power. As with Divinity itself; our eyes may not meet Thy majesty, lest we be blinded by the brilliance. We may only look upon Thee through darkened surfaces, and feel Thy heat through the great distance which separates us. Likewise, with the hidden spiritual source of creation; our souls could not confront the unspeakable glory and light.

Yet, the ancient paths of the Sun Wheel, show us the ways we must take in order to prepare and purify ourselves. Ways, which, even in this life, allow the soul to grow and obtain a state of ecstatis, which informs and gives a glimpse of the joys of that supreme state of spirit. Our journey is one of wonder and delight - of innocence and enlightenment, as we tread the Eightfold Path.

Holding their candles; the witches now tread round the Circle to the following chant:

ALL
Great is the Sun; great is his might;
following him into the light;
Feel it within; feel it without;
as joyously we sing and shout:
Glory to the God; glory to the Sun;
Catch us in Thy hands and make us one;
We are like the fire; burning and aflame;
As we reach on high; our birthright to attain.

(Repeat this chant *three* times)

Witches now stand silently; meditating upon the flame of their candles.

HIGH PRIESTESS
Now, hear and heed these words. Not for nothing was a fire kept continuously burning in our ancestor's stone circles. To them, it served many purposes: protection from wild animals; a means of keeping the body warm in winter, and a way of cooking their food. It is said that nine virgins kept a vigil over the fire and never allowed it to go out. Thus, it was a truly magical thing. Three of them tended the fire, three searched for fuel, while the remaining three rested. Gods and men lived very closely together and each shared the other's perils and joys. Religion and everyday life were one. Take this physical fire; follow it though to its inner dimensions and you will perceive it as pure energy. One or other of its aspects is at the core of every star and in the heart of every man. Evoke this most primeval of all elements, within ye.

MAGICAL WORK IS NOW PERFORMED, IF WILLED.

Closing

Circle chant

ALL
O! Magical Fire;
Through thee we aspire;
To grant us re-birth;
On our Mother Earth.
As boon-fires of old;
Their stories unfold;
To regenerate;
To make us feel great.
On hills as of yore;
Thy flames we adore;
With wills all as one;
We reach to the Sun.

(Repeat this chant *three* times)

HIGH PRIEST
What are the things that make us feel big?

ALL
Flags, flax, fodder and frig!

Server sounds the horn.

HIGH PRIEST
Guard thy light well; it is the living symbol and thyne own soul. Now, pause and contemplate: let only thy highest aspirations be dwelt upon.

The Circle is now silent for at least five minutes. At end, Server sounds the Horn again to indicate the change in consciousness.

HIGH PRIEST
Go now forward in the light.

18   The Rite of Venus

Day	Friday.
Incense or perfume	Stephanotis; apple blossom; musk; saffron; verbena; damiana (aphrodisiac herb).
Wood	Myrtle.
Colour	Light blue; pale green or pink.
Influences	All love matters; affections; partnerships; sex; spiritual harmony; compassion; friendships; offspring.

The Rite of Venus is an excellent one for promoting affection and rapport between members of the coven. Having said that, it is well to consider the formidable range of emotions which may come into being. I say formidable because the powers of Venus range from the very highest spiritual love to the most ugly and unpleasant carnal variety, which can possess a person, body, mind and soul - with the most dire consequences.

It is well to consider the true intent of the rite, and to note these widely diverse aspects of Venus, via her rulership of the signs Taurus and Libra, in which they are expressed. Venus is No 3, in the Tarot, the bringer forth of new life; hence any work connected with the reproductive powers of Nature, in any form, is permissible in this rite. The Empress is depicted with the sigil of Venus upon her shield and holds a phallic symbol, the Great Mother, Herself!

The lighting in this ritual should be very soft; possibly a rose-pink glow could be obtained through the use of a suitably coloured lamp. One candle being sufficient light on the altar.

This rite calls for partners, and these may be of the same gender according to availability and/or preference.

Erect the Circle

If possible, the witches stand alternately, male and female, round the Circle. When ready, the High Priestess strikes a sweet-toned bell six times.

HIGH PRIESTESS
Whisper to our hearts O! Gentle Goddess; creep into our souls and fill us with delight. Shine Thy lustrous light upon us, Thy children. May this long endure and our eyes shine forth that same lustre as we gaze on one another.

Females now take two steps forward and turn to face the males; (making *two* circles). They hold their hands out to the man in front of them and kiss him on both cheeks, left and right. They repeat this action with all males, going deosil round the Circle. High Priest and High Priestess included.

High Priestess strikes the Bell three times.

HIGH PRIESTESS
Approach now, the man of your choice and grant him the token of your lips.

Females go up to the male witch of their choice, embrace him and kiss him on the lips. The couples then link hands and circle deosil to the following words:

ALL
Blessed, blessed, blessed are we - to share the Dove.
Precious, precious, precious it be - from Her above.
Caring, caring, caring, go we - with perfect Love.
(Repeat, *three* times)

Each couple now goes forward, in turn, to the altar. They bow, then raising their arms and with hands still clasped, they pass by it, one on either side. When all have performed this action, they reform the circle, still keeping in couples.

High Priestess moves behind the altar and stands in the Goddess position, with hands supporting her breasts.

High Priest kneels and gives her the fivefold salute, then moves to the front of the altar, so that it is now between them. He invokes by making a 'fig' with his hand (mano in fica), and drawing the invoking pentacle before her.

HIGH PRIEST
Come to us O! Thou with the curling hips, white flesh and golden hair. Torment us with Thy wanton gaze, under winged brows. Let us glimpse the passion in Thy sea-blue eyes, and feel Thy warm and honeyed breath upon us. O! give us Thy lips of scarlet hue, moistened by the rose-pink snake of voluptuousness, which slithers from its lair of pearls and beckons us, as lecherous as a stoat.

Ivory are Thy arms which frame Thy beauteous breasts; twin peaks which the Sun did ravish 'ere he sought his rest. My eyes are dazzled by Thy splendour, O! magnificent One. Thy dark goat-mask of hair betrays Thy hidden Mystery. The silken veil which conceals the centre of all existence - the core of every star. I bow before Thee and give Thee due honour. I kiss Thy feet where jewelled flowers spring, in pursuit of Thee. Thy perfume is sweeter than Thy most exotic bloom. Hail! Hail! Hail! Venus, Star of the Evening!

ALL
Hail! Hail! Hail! Venus, Star of the Evening!

(The above invocation should be delivered with as much fervour as possible; as if speaking to the Goddess Herself)

176

HIGH PRIESTESS
Give me my Sistrum that I may stir the Winds and make Thy breath to quicken, likewise.

Server or Maiden hands sistrum to the High Priestess with a kiss.

High Priestess begins to dance with sistrum, moving round the Circle. The Dance should be performed with voluptuous movements. If the High Priestess is not accomplished in this art, she should practise some movements before the rite, although the invocation should work its own magic upon her. Suitable music may be played, if desired.

When the Dance is finished, the High Priestess resumes her place at the North of the Circle, and stands in pentacle position, symbolizing the manifested powers which have been invoked.

This is the sign for all to dance freely as they will.

MAGICAL WORK NOW TAKES PLACE, IF WILLED.

Closing

HIGH PRIESTESS
The Rite is done, and all made One. Now let us fill the Cup, that all may drink a toast to the Goddess of Love and Joy.

High Priest fills the cup, or horn, with wine. He gives it to the High Priestess, who blesses it:

HIGH PRIESTESS
O! thou wondrous vessel, which like unto She is ever overflowing with love and compassion. Be thou our guide and companion through this life, that we, likewise, may so be filled. Holiest Receiver, Bounteous One. Giver of life from the

Womb of Time. Grant us Thy blessings, so that our bodies be truly a part of Thee. *So mote it be!*

High Priestess drinks from the cup and gives it to the High Priest, who partakes likewise. He then passes it round the Circle. Each witch gives it to the next with the words:

'From me to thee; *So mote it be.*'

HIGH PRIEST
Sisters of the Blood, embrace now thy Priestess, that the powers invoked through her may dwell within ye all.

Females embrace the High Priestess, one by one, then return to their partners, embracing them in a similar manner.

HIGH PRIESTESS
Now my Star is shining bright;
In this Circle of true light;
Flashing pink and blue it gleams,
Brightest Star of all our dreams.

Kindle love within our hearts;
'Ere this Wheel of Witches parts;
Give the same to growing seeds,
Goddess Green, of all our needs.

Server strikes bell for close of Rite.

19 The Rite of Mercury

Day	Wednesday.
Incense or perfume	Sweet pea; lavender; mastic; cloves; cinnamon; cinquefoil.
Wood	Hazel.
Colour	Pale yellow.
Influences	Conjurations; predictions; knowledge; writing; eloquence; speech; speed; improvement of mind power; poetry; inspiration; healing of nervous disorders (not diseases).

The Rite of Mercury should be performed with alertness and attention. The mind is the important territory here. The body must be poised, as if ready for flight. The seers of the Circle, quick to receive any communications from the 'Messenger of the Gods.' This is the rite, *par excellence*, for attuning the mind, better speech, and stirring the imagination. The Air is Mercury's sphere which is symbolized by his winged cap and shoes. The ability to rise to any level, spiritually and mentally. Secrecy, too, is necessary. Mercury's cloak of concealment shows the adage of 'a still tongue keeping a wise head', the most difficult law in Magic: *to keep silent.*

Wisdom cannot be attained by the reading of books, or tuition of any kind. Wisdom is born of folly or age; it cannot be bought. Mercury's finger points the way - upwards. When placed against the lips, the index finger is also used for silence or as an admonishment to a naughty child. The bridge *can* be crossed; the mind *can* be trained to that state of consciousness where it is 'at one' with the Gods.

179

Keeping young at heart is a blessing (the young Dionysus was given into Mercury's care). Innocence is a peculiar virtue. This, too, is a 'gift of the Gods', a gift of Mercury, bestowing protection for the soul, an attribute of priceless worth, which the soul can carry with it into incarnation. Those who are blessed in this way cannot be corrupted by this world's evils.

Mercury connects with No 1 in the Tarot, the Magician; showing that all action has its origins in the mind which links with the Universal Mind, from whence comes all physical and material manifestation.

Erect the Circle

The Rite begins with the Server (or Maiden) sounding the horn *five* times. (The breath should be controlled so that the tone is not too loud.) The witches then link hands and begin to move round the Circle, deosil. Very slowly at first; then building up gradually until they achieve as much speed as possible.

ALL
The Horn, the Horn, we hear the Horn; sounding shrill and sweet;
The note, the note, we hear the note; compelling us to meet.
Arise, arise, we must arise; in body, mind and soul;
Attend, attend, we must attend; if we're to reach our goal.
Quick, quick, we must be quick; to glimpse his silver form;
Darting here and darting there, his errands to perform.
Glad, glad, our hearts are glad; to know he's on his way;
A beauteous form, with eyes of blue, and golden curls astray.
(Repeat *three* times)

HIGH PRIEST
Write a love-song, play the pipes; revel in thy mirth;
He will hear and soon attend our Circle here on Earth.
  (Raises sword from the altar)

180

By this Sword I raise; the symbol and the sign;
Of eloquence, wit and wisdom; that are Thy gifts divine.
Our will is here expressed; to follow in Thy sight;
With footsteps never faltering; upon our way of light.

High Priest carries the sword round the circle to every person,
who salutes it by kissing the blade. He then returns to the
centre of the circle and stands with sword raised.

HIGH PRIEST
Whosoever wishes aid within the field of Mercury, is hereby
instructed to attend these words. Keep an open mind in all
things; be ever alert and ready to learn. Scoff not at other
people's words. If they speak truth, thou art the fool. If they
speak no sense, they are teaching thee sense. Remember,
there are greater and lesser souls than thee, greater and
lesser intellects than thyne. Measure thy progress only, by
thyne own patience with ignorance and thy respect for
competence. Every soul and star is aspiring in its essence.
Each struggling onward as best it might. The Age of Aquarius
will bring new cosmic impulses to birth: the realisation that
every man must be his own saviour. Responsibility for his own
actions will be inevitable for man's spiritual development in
the Cosmos. In each new Age an appropriate zodiacal impulse
is released and becomes fixed in the subconscious mind,
where it finds fertile soil to manifest itself in the world. The
Piscean 'word' was 'At-one-ment', meaning to attain spiritual
rapport with Godhead; the two fishes, dove-tailed into one
another. In the Christian priest-hood, and by man's greed for
power and wealth, it became its exact opposite; renunciation
of responsibility in both mind and body; an easy way out!
Karmic burdens were thus made heavier; absolution of sins
bred profligacy. Man became dependent on priest for his soul.
Church preying on man for material gain. As the Piscean Age
draws to its close, the fish-scales are dropping from man's
eyes. He is at last beginning to think for himself again, and
the 'message' is becoming clear to many.

The Aquarian 'word' might well be *Tolerance*; of ourselves and others. Look deeper into this attribute; there is more here than you think. It is an attribute which breeds self-realisation; examination, and thus responsibility for one's entire structure, physical, mental and spiritual.

(High Priest slowly replaces the sword upon the altar)

HIGH PRIESTESS
While the mind is brooding upon the wisdom of those words, a chance is given to objectify thyne own aspirations, in Mercury's form.

Server takes a silver salver from the altar. This has pieces of paper and a pen upon it. He presents this to every member in turn, who will write their own personal hopes on a piece of paper; fold it up and replace it on the salver. This part of the rite should be unhurried, with no sense of 'keeping the next person waiting'. The petitions should be put in as concise a form as possible.

High Priestess approaches each person with a lighted candle, in anticipation of the Server.

HIGH PRIESTESS
May this candle be; a beacon unto ye;
As was in days of old; the spirit to behold.

High Priestess repeats these words to every member and waits on them with the candle, until they have written their petition. When all have finished; the High Priestess holds the candle for the High Priest, and vice versa. Finally, it is replaced upon the altar.

Server raises the salver of petitions.

HIGH PRIESTESS
Here are the visions of our minds; as babes new born, they are our entire responsibility! Do we dare to give them life?

ALL
We dare!

HIGH PRIESTESS
Then so be it! Who dares not, wins not. We have born them and now we must release them to do their work on Inner Levels.

Server gives the salver to the High Priestess, then brings the cauldron into the centre of the Circle. High Priestess places the papers in it.

HIGH PRIESTESS
Go thou all into Mercury's care, with safety and with light.
Grow and flower with fragrance rare, from out the darkest night.

High Priest lights the fire in the cauldron, with a taper from the altar candle. As the flames spring up the High Priestess and High Priest join the ring of witches. The High Priestess whispers a word into the ear of the witch on her left. As each witch receives it they add one word to it, before passing it on to the next person. It should be a presentable sentence of some import by the time it returns to the High Priestess. It may even be of great value to the Circle. However, the High Priestess announces the entire sentence to the coven. This may be repeated as many times as desired.

MAGICAL WORK NOW TAKES PLACE.

Closing

Circle Chant

ALL
Fire in the Cauldron; fire in the brain;
In-spi-ra-tion is Thy name.
Twisting snakes of black and white;
Uphold Thy Rod, unto our sight.

Healing powers to us bring,
Beauty bright in everything.
Silver flash - poetic art;
Mercury - to us impart.

Messenger of light divine,
Shining in our sacred shrine;
To Thee our praises we do sing;
Dancing in this Wiccan Ring.
(Repeat *three* times)

20 The Rite of the Moon

Day	Monday.
Incense or	White poppy; white rose; wallflower; myrtle;
perfume	mugwort; camphor; cedar.
Wood	Willow.
Colour	Silver or white.
Influences	Agriculture; domestic life; medicine; travel; visions; luck; feminine aspects; water; birth; time; theft (New Moon); emotions.

The Rite should be performed with the understanding that the Moon is the ruler of the Astral Plane. The Moon also controls all fluids; in humans as well as in Nature. Flux is the key-word; ebb and flow; dark and light; full and empty; *change*, in all its forms. Men as well as women have changes in their bodies, which the Moon controls. The Moistener, as she was known, was once thought to control man's fortunes too; as she changes from her brightness at Full, to disappear from sight, at the end of a month.

The New Moon; The Silver Huntress; Maiden of the Mysteries. *The Full Moon* - the Mother; when she reflects the Sun's light fully and his taking of her; Queen of Heaven. *The Waning Moon* - the Old One; rocking in her chair; sliding low in the sky, when all 'good' folk are safely abed. Keeper of our most secret inner thoughts, knowing, cunning. So the Moon reflects and rules human emotions, sexual urges, and on a higher level, the imagination and subconscious mind. In the Tarot, the Moon is numbered 18. One plus eight equals nine; and nine is the number of the Moon. Among other things, the card shows the glamour and compulsion the Moon has upon the animal kingdom, and although man also feels these urges, the path from the water to the distant mountains tells him his goal is yet beyond the Moon and her allure.

The appreciation and experience which the Moon gives can be of great benefit to the initiate, yet they are not the goal. Likewise, the gifts of clairvoyance and clairaudience are beneficial, but are not the final accomplishments of the soul.

Erect the Circle

At the commencement of the rite, the only candles lit are the ones at the four quarters of the Circle. A mirror, or similar reflective surface, is necessary. Ideally, this should be upon the North Wall, or upon the altar itself.

The members stand silently, round the Circle. The High Priestess takes up the sistrum and shakes it nine times. She now lights the first altar candle, which is coloured *red*.

The Maiden, or a female younger than the High Priestess, next comes forward and lights the second altar candle; which is coloured *white*.

The third female, older than the High Priestess, lights the last candle, a *black* or *dark-blue* one. Together, they raise the candles so that they are reflected in the mirror, and *hold* the position. Then slowly they turn to face the south, still holding their candles (backs to altar).

During the above actions, the three witches should meditate and identify with the particular aspect of the Moon they are representing.

MAIDEN
Chaste am I when first you see
The silver bow behind the tree.

In this state all men come to me;
The essence of my Mystery!

HIGH PRIESTESS
Fecund giver of life am I,
Yet all who live are bound to die.
Perfection is shown in me to be
The Mother of all on land and sea.

I rule the tides of death and birth
For all who dwell on this brood Earth.
Fear not the future of thy Fate;
Thy end will see another Gate!

CRONE
I, the dark one, now behold
All thy secrets I enfold.
If my image thou canst bear;
And the Abyss thou wilt dare;
The Silver Path will then be thyne
To lead thee to my sacred shrine.

ALL THREE
Three in One and One in Three:
The oldest form of Trinity.
Goddess Triformis; the Mothers, we;
Isis - Rhea and Binah Ge!

The Mothers now turn to the altar and place their candles
upon it, white on left, red in centre, dark-blue on right.

The Mothers form a small circle in front of the altar and circle
three times. Then linking hands, they circle *three* times.
Finally, they circle *three* times, with arms round each other's
waists.

The Maiden now takes up the scourge from the altar; the High Priestess picks up her red candle, while the Crone lifts up the athame. Each hold their symbols up in one hand, while a single pillar is made by standing close together. High Priestess facing front, Maiden to right and Crone to left. Their free arms should be closely linked. *They hold position.*

ALL
Hail Moon Mother, Goddess Hail!
Great One of the night, All Hail!
Dark to light and light to dark;
Cross the sky a-turning;
We on Earth do understand,
Our faith in Thee, affirming.

Show us in Thy silver beams,
Life in all its meaning,
Guiding us in Nature's ways,
Mistress of our dreaming.

Ruler of the hearth and home,
Lady of the tides,
All our days are blessed by Thee
While this Earth abides.

When the Silver Cord is cut
In the Astral light,
The River we shall cross to Thee
Once more into Thy sight.
So mote it be.

The Mothers lay their symbols back upon the altar and stand with linked hands. Server fills the Cup with water and presents it to the High Priest: who holds it up to the Mothers.

HIGH PRIEST
Queen of the Night, I pray Thee bless this, Thyne element of
Water, most precious fluid of Life.

High Priestess takes the Cup, while the Maiden and Crone
kneel, one on either side, facing each other. All three raise
Cup and *hold position*.

HIGH PRIESTESS
We bless this fluid and consecrate it in the name of the Magna
Mater.

MAIDEN
Let it be filled with purity and love.

CRONE
Give all who partake therein Inspiration and Wisdom.

High Priest receives Cup and drinks from it. He is followed by
all the coven. The Mothers drink last, and give the Cup to the
Server who replaces it upon the altar.

The Mothers now join the others and lead the Dance to the
following:

ALL
Flowing - Increasing - Light,
Bearing - Filling - Bright,   (Deosil)
Receiving - Giving - Delight.

Ebbing - Waning - Fading,
Secrets - Ever - Hiding,   (Widdershins)
Darkness - Mystery - Shrouding.   Anti-clockwise

Flowing - Increasing - Light,
Bearing - Filling - Bright,   (Deosil)
Receiving - Giving - Delight.

(Repeat *each* verse *three* times, reversing direction of Dance,
as written above)

PERFORMANCE OF MAGICAL WORK. IF WILLED.

Closing

High Priest steps into centre of Circle.

HIGH PRIEST
Come to the image of the Moon;
Look into her face;
Revelations she may show
By her especial grace.

Memories of another mask
Thy soul has worn before;
Symbols, signs and omens,
That Fate has yet in store.

One by one the witches approach the Magic Mirror and scry
in it for a time. If willed, this may be followed by as many as
wish, scrying in their own individual speculums. Any results
should of course, be recorded.

The Server takes a cauldron or vessel filled with water, from
under the altar and places it in the centre of Circle.

The following chant is lead by the Mothers. The Dance should
be performed with linked hands, the pace being *steady* and
graceful:

ALL
O! Moon of moods we follow thee, in the dark night shining;
Filling us with visions rare, Mistress of our dreaming.
Draw us in thyne argent beam, through the Horned Gate;
So we may come nigh to thee, Lady of our Fate.

In the darkened surface, of water or of glass,
Past or present may be glimpsed, and things to come to pass.
Lunar enchantment manifold, of love in all its faces,
Appearing when we least suspect, in the most unlikely places.
The Waters of Life thou freely give, when rocking in the
    womb,
Ruler of birth and re-birth, from cradle and the tomb.
Nine is the number of thyne orb, nine is the number clear,
Nine are the Moons it takes of thee, for new life to appear.
Goddess of the Silver Bow, Mistress of the Chase,
Lady, pure thou art to all, for few may see thy face.

Server fills the Cup with water, taken from a decanter and gives it to the High Priest, who addresses the High Priestess:

HIGH PRIEST
Lady of Light, bless for us this lunar fluid, that we may be made One in its Mystery.

(Gives Cup to High Priestess)

HIGH PRIESTESS
Be this sacred water consecrate; may all who bathe therein be blessed and cleansed. May the rain-bow of beauty shine o'er them, even as the veil of rain transforms the light of the Sun into an arc of miraculous colours. *Come!*

High Priestess empties the Cup into the cauldron. The witches approach separately, in the following order: Maiden, Crone, High Priest, Server, and members. They are asperged from the cauldron by the High Priestess. High Priest asperges High Priestess, last.

All form circle holding hands, approach cauldron and kneeling, plunge their *linked* hands into the water.

Appendix: The Sequence of the Planetary Periods

Day
Sunrise to Sunset

Sunday	Monday	Tuesday	Wednesday
1 Sun	Moon	Mars	Mercury
2 Venus	Saturn	Sun	Moon
3 Mercury	Jupiter	Venus	Saturn
4 Moon	Mars	Mercury	Jupiter
5 Saturn	Sun	Moon	Mars
6 Jupiter	Venus	Saturn	Sun
7 Mars	Mercury	Jupiter	Venus
8 Sun	Moon	Mars	Mercury
9 Venus	Saturn	Sun	Moon
10 Mercury	Jupiter	Venus	Saturn
11 Moon	Mars	Mercury	Jupiter
12 Saturn	Sun	Moon	Mars

Thursday	Friday	Saturday
1 Jupiter	Venus	Saturn
2 Mars	Mercury	Jupiter
3 Sun	Moon	Mars
4 Venus	Saturn	Sun
5 Mercury	Jupiter	Venus
6 Moon	Mars	Mercury
7 Saturn	Sun	Moon
8 Jupiter	Venus	Saturn
9 Mars	Mercury	Jupiter
10 Sun	Moon	Mars
11 Venus	Saturn	Sun
12 Mercury	Jupiter	Venus

Night
Sunset to Sunrise

Sunday	Monday	Tuesday	Wednesday
1 Jupiter	Venus	Saturn	Sun
2 Mars	Mercury	Jupiter	Venus
3 Sun	Moon	Mars	Mercury
4 Venus	Saturn	Sun	Moon
5 Mercury	Jupiter	Venus	Saturn
6 Moon	Mars	Mercury	Jupiter
7 Saturn	Sun	Moon	Mars
8 Jupiter	Venus	Saturn	Sun
9 Mars	Mercury	Jupiter	Venus
10 Sun	Moon	Mars	Mercury
11 Venus	Saturn	Sun	Moon
12 Mercury	Jupiter	Venus	Saturn

Thursday	Friday	Saturday
1 Moon	Mars	Mercury
2 Saturn	Sun	Moon
3 Jupiter	Venus	Saturn
4 Mars	Mercury	Jupiter
5 Sun	Moon	Mars
6 Venus	Saturn	Sun
7 Mercury	Jupiter	Venus
8 Moon	Mars	Mercury
9 Saturn	Sun	Moon
10 Jupiter	Venus	Saturn
11 Mars	Mercury	Jupiter
12 Sun	Moon	Mars

Bíblíography

Bracelin, J.L., *Gerald Gardner: Witch*. (Octagon Press, 1960)

Brewer, Rev. Dr., *The Guide to English History*. (Jarrold & Sons) (no date or initials given)

Connon, F. Wallace, *The Stone of Destiny*. (The Covenant Publishing Co., Ltd., 1951)

Dames, Michael, *The Silbury Treasure*. (Thames & Hudson, 1976)

- *The Avebury Cycle*. (Thames & Hudson, 1977)

Gardner, Gerald B., *A Goddess Arrives*. (Arthur Stockwell Ltd.)

- *High Magic's Aid*. (Michael Houghton, 1949)

- *The Meaning of Witchcraft*. (Aquarian Press, 1959)

- *Witchcraft Today*. (Rider & Co., 1954)

- *Keris and Other Malay Weapons*. (E.P. Publishing, Yorkshire, 1973)

Graves, Robert, *The White Goddess*. (Faber & Faber, 1961)

Harrison, Michael, *The Roots of Witchcraft*. (Muller, 1973)

Hawkins, Gerald S., *Stonehenge Decoded*. (Souvenir Press, 1966)

Leslie, Shane (Editor), *Anthology of Catholic Poets*. (Macmillan Ltd.)

Lethbridge, T.C., *E.S.P., Beyond Time and Distance*. (Sidgwick & Jackson, 1974)

- *Ghosts and the Divining Rod*. (Routledge & Kegan Paul, 1963)

Michell, John, *The City of Revelation*. (Abacus, 1973)

- *The View over Atlantis*. (Abacus, 1973)

Murray, Margaret A., *The God of the Witches*. (Faber & Faber, 1952)

- *Witchcraft in Western Europe*. (OUP, 1921)

Phillips, Guy R., *Brigantia*. (Routledge & Kegan Paul, 1976)

Underwood, Guy, *The Pattern of the Past*. (Abacus, 1974)

Valiente, Doreen, *An ABC of Witchcraft*. (Robert Hale, 1973)

- *Witchcraft for Tomorrow*. (Robert Hale, 1978)

Vogh, James, *Arachne Rising*. (Hart-Davis/MacGibbon, 1977)

Waddell, L.A., *Phoenician Origin of Britons, Scots and Anglo-Saxons*. (William & Norgate Ltd., 1924)

Walton, Evangeline, *The Island of the Mighty (and Other Legends)*. (Pan/Ballantine, 1970)

Watkins, Alfred, *The Old Straight Track*. (Abacus, 1974)

Index

A selection of other Capall Bann titles. Free catalogue available.

Seasonal Magic - Diary of a Village Witch by Paddy Slade

This book is about seasonal magic, that is, the stuff used by country witches. It is of the earth. This is a distillation of old wisdom from the heart, without pretence, without a need to 'get a message across'. Rites for the festivals (including Paddy's famous Rite of Chocolate - an experience not to be missed!), animal and herb lore, spells, chants, recipes, folk remedies, snippets of knowledge and a candid view of the witches world are all here, written with humour, genuine knowledge and a deep love of the subject itself, by a bona fide 'village witch'. ISBN 1898307 94 6   £10.95

Patchwork of Magic - Living In a Pagan World   by Julia Day

A patchwork is composed of numerous coloured pieces, sewn together to make something beautiful and practical. This book contains many experiences, facts, thoughts and ideas to consider. It has a light-hearted look at some of the facets of Pagan life and compares different subdivisions which have formed within that world, attempting to make sense of groups as diverse as Druids and Chaos workers, examing diverse aspects such as making incense and carrying out acts of magic during everyday activities. Help with personal development is also given in matters such as grounding, centring, learning from dreams, recognising synchronicity in your life and living an increasingly magical and Pagan life. This book combines the natural energies of Earth and Sky, sewn together with love and a fair bit of laughter. ISBN 1898 307210   £9.95

In Search of Herne the Hunter by Eric Fitch

Commences with an introduction to Herne's story, the oak on which Herne hanged himself & its significance in history & mythology. Goes on to investigates antlers & their symbology in prehistoric religions, with a study of the horned god Cernunnos, the Wild Hunt & its associations with Woden, Herne & the Christian devil & a descriptive chapter on the tradition of dressing up as animals & the wearing & use of antlers in particular. Herne's suicide & its connection with Woden & prehistoric sacrifice is covered, together with the most complete collection of Herne's appearances, plus an investigation into the nature of his hauntings. Photographs, illustrations & diagrams enhance the text. ISBN 1898307 237   £9.95

The Goddess Year by Nigel Pennick and Helen Field

A celebration of the sacred female throughout the Pagan year. Nigel writes the text which describes the changes and progressions within the year cycle, sacred days and festivals of various Goddesses within the tradition and how the appropriate day relates to them. There are new time-wheels throughout the book, which has eight sections, there are sections relating to the major eight festivals and the Goddess Days of the Moon, with texts on the corresponding nine Goddesses. Superb illustrations illuminate the richly researched text. ISBN 1898307 636   £10.95

West Country Wicca - A Journal of the Old Religion by Rhiannon Ryall

A simple account of the Old Religion. There is no "title" for this system since the author was taught before the current revival groups formed. The portrayal of Wicca in the olden days is at once charming & deeply religious, combining joy, simplicity & reverence. Wisdom shines forth from the pages of this book, the wisdom emanating from country folk who live close to Nature & a wisdom which can add depth & colour to our present day understanding of the Craft. Without placing more value on her way than ours, Rhiannon provides us with a direct path back to the Old Religion in the British Isles. Her writing is like the conversation of an old family friend, warm & familiar as that of a dear relative. ISBN 1898307 024   £7.95

FREE DETAILED CATALOGUE

A detailed illustrated catalogue is available on request, SAE or International Postal Coupon appreciated. **Titles can be ordered direct from Capall Bann, post free in the UK** (cheque or PO with order) or from good bookshops and specialist outlets. Titles currently available include:

Angels and Goddesses - Celtic Christianity & Paganism by Michael Howard
Arthur - The Legend Unveiled by C Johnson & E Lung
Auguries and Omens - The Magical Lore of Birds by Yvonne Aburrow
Caer Sidhe - Celtic Astrology and Astronomy by Michael Bayley
Call of the Horned Piper by Nigel Jackson
Cats' Company by Ann Walker
Celtic Lore & Druidic Ritual by Rhiannon Ryall
Compleat Vampyre - The Vampyre Shaman: Werewolves & Witchery by Nigel Jackson
Crystal Clear - A Guide to Quartz Crystal by Jennifer Dent
Earth Dance - A Year of Pagan Rituals by Jan Brodie
Earth Harmony - Places of Power, Holiness and Healing by Nigel Pennick
Earth Magic by Margaret McArthur
Enchanted Forest - The Magical Lore of Trees by Yvonne Aburrow
Familiars - Animal Powers of Britain by Anna Franklin
Healing Homes by Jennifer Dent
Herbcraft - Shamanic & Ritual Use of Herbs by Susan Lavender & Anna Franklin
In Search of Herne the Hunter by Eric Fitch
Magical Incenses and Perfumes by Jan Brodie
Magical Lore of Cats by Marion Davies
Magical Lore of Herbs by Marion Davies
Masks of Misrule - The Horned God & His Cult in Europe by Nigel Jackson
Mysteries of the Runes by Michael Howard
Patchwork of Magic by Julia Day
Psychic Self Defence - Real Solutions by Jan Brodie
Runic Astrology by Nigel Pennick
Sacred Animals by Gordon MacLellan
Sacred Grove - The Mysteries of the Forest by Yvonne Aburrow
Sacred Geometry by Nigel Pennick
Sacred Lore of Horses The by Marion Davies
Sacred Ring - Pagan Origins British Folk Festivals & Customs by Michael Howard
Seasonal Magic - Diary of a Village Witch by Paddy Slade
Secret Places of the Goddess by Philip Heselton
Talking to the Earth by Gordon Maclellan
Taming the Wolf - Full Moon Meditations by Steve Hounsome
The Goddess Year by Nigel Pennick & Helen Field
West Country Wicca by Rhiannon Ryall

Capall Bann is owned and run by people actively involved in many of the areas in which we publish. Our list is expanding rapidly so do contact us for details on the latest releases.

Capall Bann Publishing, Auton Farm, Milverton, Somerset TA4 1NE